The Going Was Good

The Going Was Good

Memoir of a Transatlantic Life

DAVID BUISSERET

ARPress
ILLUMINATING IDEAS
EMPOWERING VOICES

ARPress
45 Dan Road Suite 5
Canton MA 02021
Hotline: 1(888) 821-0229
Fax: 1(508) 545-7580

Ordering Information:
Quantity sales. Special discounts are available on quantity purchases by corporations, associations, and others. For details, contact the publisher at the address above.

Printed in the United States of America.

ISBN-13:   Softcover   979-8-89389-582-7
            eBook   979-8-89389-583-4

Library of Congress Control Number: 2024920910

In Loving Memory of
Dr. Paul Buisseret, 1974-2018

Table of Contents

Preface

Entering upon the vainglorious business of composing a memoir is tricky. Whom is it for? The children, friends, former colleagues or who? In the end, one simply hopes that the family will bear with the "professional" chapters, and that other people will not be vexed by periodic intrusions by the family. I take refuge in the reflection of Sir Richard Steele, once editor of *The Tatler*:" it is to be noted that when any part of this paper appears dull, there is a design in it." Perhaps chapter 10, on the Newberry Library, will try the patience of non-professional readers most sorely.

In composing this memoir, I have been able to call on a variety of sources. My Belgian grandfather kept a small "black book," in which he jotted down the main lines of the Buisserets from the eighteenth century onwards. Of course, in the days of computerized genealogy it is now possible to go back much further than that; indeed, to the late fifteenth century. The Buisserets of the Sambre valley, sometimes subject to the king of France and sometimes to the Habsburg emperor, were small nobles, who over the centuries contrived neither to slide into the peasantry nor to distinguish themselves in the wider world, except for one Counter-Reformation bishop. As well as the black book, I had a long set of my own appointment-books, dating from 1952 until the present. These reminded me of what was happening year by year, and some of them contained documents of interest, like the ticket to a (cricket) Test Match at Sabina Park, Jamaica, in 1965 (chapter 9, plate 21).

In addition, I have long kept what used to be called a "commonplace book," in which I noted phrases and poems which had particularly caught my fancy. Finally, for many years (before email) some of the children were diligent in keeping in touch with us, and their letters make up a precious source. For images, we have like many families a long set of albums, and these also play an important role in bringing distant times to life; indeed, the temptation is to make too much use of them.

Several friends have helped with this memoir. John Roach, my former tutor at Cambridge, made many helpful suggestions early on, as did Eddie (Pratapaditya) Pal of Los Angeles, and Jennifer Robertson of Raleigh. So did several of the children; Claire also largely succeeded in bringing some Yankee order to my punctuation. I had in the end to urge them to remember what Lord Balfour once remarked to Winston Churchill, then a member of his Cabinet: "Winston, I always admire the exaggerated way you tell the truth." A good point to bear in mind...

Chicago, July 2016

For this second edition, I have made a few corrections and additions, following the advice of various friends.

Chicago, June 2021

1

The Isle of Wight, 1934-1940

One side of this story has a very romantic beginning. My paternal Belgian grandfather, Arthur Buisseret (1860-1936), had come to London about 1880, after his studies at the Collège d'Enghien, in Louvain; in those days, Europeans could travel and work freely between various countries. He had been appointed organist at the English Martyrs' Church, just by Tower Hill in East London, a church founded in 1866 by the Italian Oblate Fathers in order to look after some of the many families of Irish immigrants (often refugees from the famines of the 1840s) who lived in that depressed part of London. Eventually, my wife and I were to realize that we were both, in a manner of speaking, children of the Irish diaspora, both with grandmothers characteristically called "Julia."

Arthur lodged by the church at 30 Great Prescot Street, in a house which can still be seen (1); there he shared the lodgings with a large Irish family of ten children. The youngest was called Julia O'Halloran, and she used to help her father, who was a tailor. In the course of this work, Julia sometimes dropped on the common stairs golden threads from the work that she carried for her father. Passing the same way, Arthur apparently made a bouquet of the threads, and one day presented then to her, thus winning her heart.

(1) English Martyrs' Church and the house at 30 Great Prescot Street, in East London. Both survived the Blitz intact; a bomb fell through the roof of the church but failed to explode.

The young pair were married in the English Martyrs' Church in August 1883, and at first lived in London, where Arthur, the exact contemporary of Sir Edward Elgar, continued his organ-playing and some teaching; he also became a representative of the Pearl Life Insurance Company. This was a relatively novel kind of business venture in which he eventually became quite prosperous. Arthur and Julia soon found life in London bad for their health – these were the days of dense "pea-soups," when the choking fog could make it hard to see across the street – and in 1886 they moved first to Gosport, near Portsmouth on the south coast, and then to Newport, in the center of the Isle of Wight (2). Arthur continued his work in insurance, and for a while taught at Newport Grammar School.

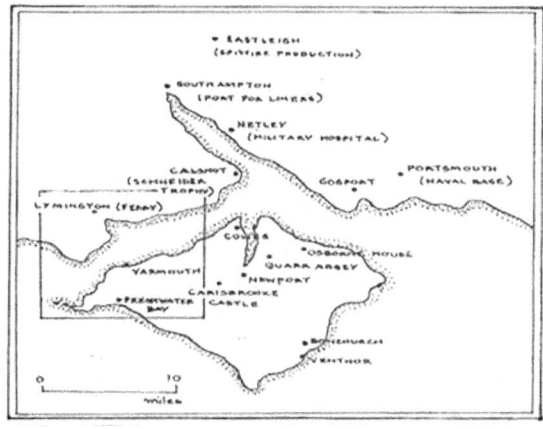

(2) The Isle of Wight and the nearby mainland. Large ships from Southampton generally went out into the Channel to the east of the Island, as the passage by the Needles could be tricky.

Three years later, with three children, the young family moved to the west end of the Island, at Totland Bay, and here Arthur founded the "St. Joseph's Secondary School" (3), on a small hill not far from the sea. It looks as if the postcard shows him and Julia outside the front of the house, by the steps leading down to the tennis-court; there they had a Lourdes grotto. As the school prospered, a large addition was made, with fresh classrooms and some dormitories. This addition had to be heavily buttressed against the southwesterly gales which would sweep up out of the English Channel.

(3) A postcard showing St. Joseph's shortly after its construction, about 1890. Arthur is on the steps, and Julia on the tennis-court; there was ample room for a vegetable garden to the right.

Arthur had come to the Island at a time when it had a certain national importance. It was the young Queen Victoria and her consort Prince Albert who began a new phase in its history, when in 1840 they decided to build a home at Osborne House, near Ryde. Her frequent presence there meant that large numbers of fashionable people were drawn to the Island; Napoleon III and his empress in 1857, for instance. People began to build elegant houses all over the Island, to which artists and writers like Charles Dickens and Alfred Tennyson were particularly attracted. Just across the Solent was Southampton, becoming a major port with the development of railways. Instead of sailing round to London or landing at Plymouth and taking the stage-coach, passengers could now land at Southampton and directly board fast trains to London. So the narrow strip of water between the Island and the mainland now saw a continual parade of vessels of all kinds, from battleships to ocean liners, as well as an annual regatta that became very fashionable.

Meanwhile Arthur's family continued to grow, eventually reaching nine children. They are seen on the occasion of the Silver Wedding in 1908 (4). Of the three girls, two would eventually become Franciscan nuns (as sister Égide already is), and two Benedictine priests (as Father Gregory already is). Julia is holding the youngest child, and the one on the right, below Father Gregory, is my father, Ralph (they were all also called "Joseph").

(4) A family group taken on the tennis-court, for the Silver Wedding of 1908.

Arthur seems to have been quite prosperous. For instance, he would on occasion order a cask of wine from France. When it arrived at the Totland Bay railway station, it would be carried on a cart up to Saint Joseph's, where the boys would be set to decanting the wine into bottles, which they then sealed with corks, using hammers. The boys all went away to school, though this was surely less costly than it has become; my father went to the Franciscan College at Cowley, outside Oxford.

When the First World War came, in 1914, the two Franciscan sisters remained in their Belgian convent, under German occupation. At this time, unlike 1940, they do not seem to have received the unwelcome attentions of the German occupiers. Father Gregory remained at Belmont College in England, and Father Frank served in the ill-fated 1917 expedition to Iraq, where he remembered surviving on "dates and dirty water," and being heavily reliant on an "Evinrude" motor for his boat. Of the four lay brothers, two served on the Western Front, where Edmund won the *croix de guerre*; the others, including my father, were too young to serve. The war ended in 1918 and this led to the Treaty of Versailles, which apparently Arthur condemned as being hopelessly unfair to Germany, as indeed it was; he seems to have foreseen the disastrous outcome.

After the war, Arthur continued to run the school, and the four lay brothers went their separate ways. Three of them had curiously similar lives; they all became schoolmasters, and all ended up as reserve lieutenant-colonels in some branch of the British army. Indeed, it is astonishing to reflect, now, how much of the lives of Arthur's children was taken up with preparations for war against Germany, and then in fighting in those wars. It is also curious to notice that Julia's family quite faded from the picture. Ireland seems to have been regarded as a rebellious and undesirable province, particularly after the uprising of 1916, and the Buisserets do not seem to have retained any contact with the O'Halloran family.

Arthur retired in 1931, going to live in Belgium, where he died in 1936; Julia then went to live with her daughters at their convent in Soignies. Julia was interrogated by the Gestapo after the German occupation in June 1940, but she was not detained. Perhaps Julia was saved by the intercession of her Belgian neighbors; the Gestapo would surely not have been so lenient had they known that the convent's cellars sometimes hid both Jewish people and allied airmen. Julia lived until 1946, when I can still remember the black-bordered envelope which arrived at our house in Suffolk from recently liberated Belgium.

When Arthur retired, the school was taken over by my father, Ralph. It was no light task, for in addition to four classes of local boys, Saint Joseph's had begun to take in young men from continental Europe who wanted to perfect their English. Keeping them all lodged and fed and instructed must have taken a good deal of work for a single man, even with the help of Mrs. Crode, cook and housekeeper, from the village of Freshwater Bay. In 1933, though, Ralph was joined by my mother, Margaret Hill (in the fashion of the day, they were known as "Rafe" and "Maidie").

She had been working in the Bank of England as an accounts clerk, a position which required unremitting precision and some mathematical skill, and had come to the Island on holiday, then falling in love. Her family does not seem to have approved of the union, since Ralph clearly was not very prosperous, and was not even English (or Anglican...), though he was very handsome in a sporting sort of way (5). Maidie threw herself into the running of the school, which involved many outings and picnics with the foreign students, as well as the usual drudgery involved in running a large establishment. She soon became pregnant, and in 1996, when we visited the Island, Pat and I met an old man who had been a schoolboy at St Joseph's, and had last seen me "in your mother's belly."

(5) Ralph and Maidie about 1935. They are standing by the
club house of the golf course on Afton Down.

I was born to Maidie in December of 1934 – a crucial year for Hitler - and a few days later was taken out in my pram, to breathe the invigorating winter air (6). The pram (of a wonderfully efficient kind, which allowed the baby to be peacefully rocked with one hand; it has gone out of fashion) is being held by the District Nurse, in her very elegant uniform.

(6) The District Nurse, with my mother and pram ("perambulator").

In those days before the National Health Service children were generally born at home, with the nurse acting as midwife. Indeed, I do not remember that my parents had any contact with a doctor or hospital in those days. The end of Saint Joseph's is visible, and beyond it the tennis court, on which some sheep appear to be grazing. Perhaps my mother is on her way to a delightful walk along the top of the cliffs in Totland Bay known as "The Walk;" it still survives, with wonderful views down the English Channel to the west.

English houses in those days tended to be cold in winter, so that people often wore thick woolens and tweeds inside the house (7). In this image, I am standing on some bricks that were part of a conservatory that my father was building to house a grapevine, for the Isle of Wight was notable for its mild climate, particularly on the south coast; this has become even more marked, with climate change.

(7) Mother and child, about the spring of 1936.
Heavy woolens were the dress of choice.

Traditionally, writers of memoirs try to remember their first memories, though of course these are often faulty, overladen with subsequent recollections. I seem first to remember an occasion when we had gone to watch the sailing of some new Cunard liner from Southampton, and it may have been the *Queen Mary* (8). We would have been on the seafront at Cowes, as the huge vessel slowly eased out of the Solent, bound for New York. I particularly remember the occasion, because a bee then stung me on the eyelid. Two other deep images from that time survive for me; one is of Finnish soldiers in their snowy white uniforms, putting up a valiant resistance against the Soviets, and the other is of Adolf Hitler, riding triumphantly in his great black open Mercedes through some fragrant green German pine-forest, probably in Saxony.

(8) An outing to Cowes, to see the sailing of the *Queen Mary*, about 1938. This fast liner would offer a relatively safe way to cross the Atlantic in wartime, as she could outrun all submarines.

There must have been arguments among Saint Joseph's foreign students, because some came from Germany, and others from France and Belgium, and I have sometimes wondered if some were not spies, interested in this strategic area. But they seem to have jogged by peaceably enough, enlivening the days with plenty of picnics and swimming-parties and tennis-matches. Our household seems to have been very much oriented towards gardening, which provided the vegetables for the kitchen, and sports of various kinds (my father often went away to play in games of field hockey). As well as their Scottish terrier, and they always had one from one generation to the next, my parents kept a goat, perhaps for milk (9). We never ate outside the house, except for picnics, but on one occasion I remember tasting that American delicacy, an ice-cream, at the village chemist's; it had an amazingly rich flavor that I can still remember.

(9) On the tennis court with our cat, dog and goat, probably in 1939. Alas, the flat court proved ideal for putting up ugly Nissen huts to house the float-factory during the war.

This peaceable existence came to an end with the declaration of war in 1939. The foreign students all went home, sometimes without paying their bills, and the Island began to be put on a war footing. My father joined the Home Guard, and my mother became a driver for the Saint John's Ambulance group. I remember that she took delight in speeding about the narrow lanes of the Island in this heavy vehicle. In general, I do not recall any apprehension in the air. We were at first confident that the French would resist, as they had in 1914, and even after that the English had such confidence in the Royal Navy that an invasion seemed out of the question. On foggy nights, we felt ourselves safely enveloped by the whooping of destroyers from Portsmouth as they patrolled around the Island.

After the collapse of France in June 1940, the next phase was the German attempt to destroy the Royal Air Force, in preparation for an invasion. The ensuing Battle of Britain took place right over our heads. There were many targets in the vicinity, including the docks at Southampton and Portsmouth, the Spitfire factory at Eastleigh and the radar station at Ventnor. The battle raged overhead, as the incoming Germans were engaged by the Spitfires and Hurricanes of the RAF; it was a strange feeling, to be present at such a titanic struggle, to faintly hear machine-guns, to see vapor-trails, and yet to be out of harm's way. Of course, we then had no understanding of the way in which the newly-developed radar system permitted the RAF to make the most effective interceptions of the oncoming German aircraft. Nor did we know anything of the reckless bravery of the RAF's Polish exile pilots, who would sometimes break up these bomber-formations by furiously and unconventionally attacking them head-on.

I once remember sitting in the sandpit in our playing field, with my helper Pansy from the village, when a German aircraft, probably a Messerschmitt 109 fighter, shot overhead on its way back to France, trailing whitish-brown smoke. Like so many others, it probably crashed in the English Channel, drowning the unfortunate pilot. I also remember going round the playing field one morning picking up what seemed to be harmless little cylinders with a curious smell. I now think that they must have been expended incendiary sticks, of which we made a neat pile. On another occasion, we went to Major Corfield's farm to see a huge hole made by a crashing Spitfire. Perhaps the pilot escaped, and probably the engine was buried deep in the middle of the hole, where such survivals have sometimes been recovered by excavation in recent years.

Eventually the fighting died down, and the Germans retreated to lick their wounds. My parents then went with me for Christmas 1940 to stay with her mother at Woodbridge, in Suffolk. Perhaps it was getting difficult to run Saint Joseph's, with the foreign students all gone, and many of the parents of the young pupils also leaving the Island, which was thought to be in danger of invasion. After the war, a German aerial photograph was discovered which in fact showed one of the beaches where we used to picnic, identifying it as a good place for a landing by parachute troops (10). No such attack ever came, but when they were in Woodbridge, my parents learned that Saint Joseph's had been taken over ("requisitioned" as the phrase was) by the Ministry of Aircraft Production, and that they had two weeks in which to leave.

We all hurried back to the Island and did what we could to pack up our belongings. I recall the devastation in London as we passed through by taxi, from Liverpool Street to Waterloo Stations. Even more I remember feeling on the ferry, as we slowly pulled away from the Island, that the Island was actually leaving us, a most curious sensation that I have never had again. In fact, it was correct, for Saint Joseph's was much altered by the need to produce floats for the amphibious air-sea rescue aircraft known as a "Walrus," and we were never able to return to our sadly altered home. Our future was to be in flat Suffolk, far from the Island's green and rolling downs.

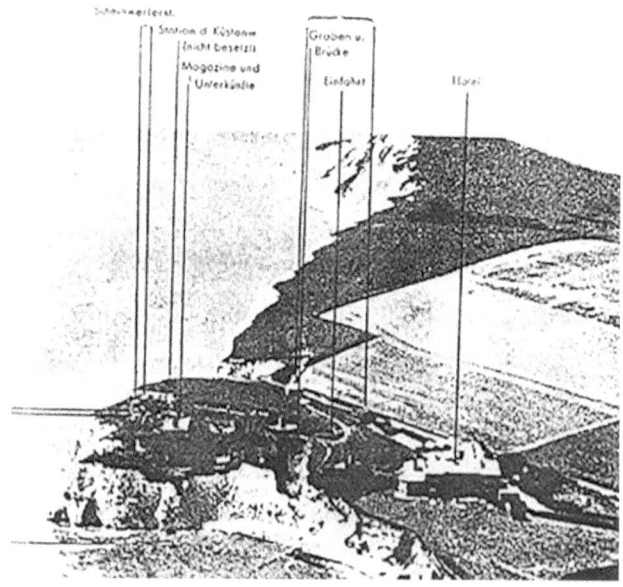

(10) German aerial photograph for paratroops of the cliffs above Freshwater Bay, where we often went for picnics. Tennyson's Down stretches away in the background, towards the Needles.

2

Growing up in Woodbridge, 1941-1952

Obliged to leave the Isle of Wight in the winter of 1940-41, we at first took refuge in Woodbridge with Almena Hill, my maternal grandmother ("Almena" was a fashionable name in the 1890s). She had grown up during the 1890s in Devonshire, where her father was Borough Engineer for Plymouth, an important British naval base. A photograph of about 1900 shows a rather willful-looking young woman (1); her family seems to have occupied a fairly prominent place in the society of the time, as in 1902 Almena was invited to attend the coronation procession of the new king, Edward VII (2).

(1) Almena Paton, probably at Plymouth about 1890.

Coronation Procession,

JUNE 27th, 1902.

45, PARLIAMENT STREET, S.W.

Admit

Miss Paton

(2) Almena's invitation to the Coronation Procession of Edward VII in 1902.

Almena lived in a solid Victorian terrace house, number 109, on Melton Hill, at the northern end of Woodbridge (3). The road in front was the old coach route between London and Lowestoft, and for some reason I could never look at it without thinking of the way the stagecoach must have lumbered up Melton Hill, on its way into town, and passed right in front of our house. Perhaps this image was so powerful for a little boy because a few hundred yards into the town was the Crown Hotel, where you could still see the courtyard where the coach must have stopped, perhaps to change horses; you could also see, round the back, where they had been stabled. Later on, when I read Charles Dickens' *Pickwick Papers*, the image took even livelier form as Dickens described his arrival at the White Horse in Ipswich, the next stage on the road to London, and his unexpected adventures there (4).

Almena had inklings of a former age about her. For instance, she liked to hum the old music-hall song whose chorus was "Oh Mr. porter, what shall I do; I wanted to go to Birmingham and they've taken me on to Crewe. So, take me back to Birmingham as quickly as you can; Oh Mr. porter, what a silly girl I am." Also, when I poured her a "whisky-mack," her favourite drink, she always told me to shake the bottle against "the fusel-oil." When we much later visited a distillery in Scotland, I learned that this was a potentially dangerous substance found in home-distilled whisky. The Patons came from Scotland, and Almena's advice no doubt survived from an illegal still.

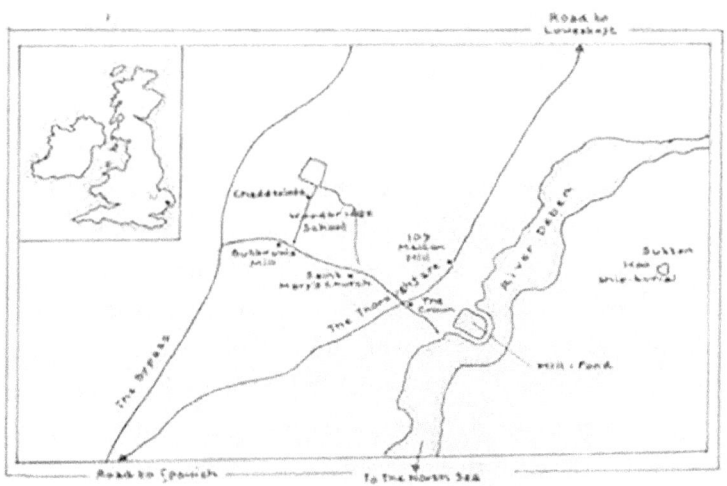

(3) Sketch-map to show the places mentioned in the text.

(4) Drawing of a nineteenth-century stagecoach breasting a hill.

In those days there was an unpaved lane at the back of 109 Melton Hill, and at the end of this lane lived the local vet, Dr. Heatley. In the lane my father would sometimes "decoke" his Morris car's engine, which involved removing the top of the engine block, scraping out the carbon deposits, and then replacing the block with a new gasket (engines used to purr like sewing-machines after that). On one occasion, probably in the summer of 1941, I was watching my father at this task when an MG tourer (a "convertible") came down the lane to the vet's house. His son was driving it, and I remember my father remarking, quite unusually, "that's Heatley's son; he's a clever bloke." I do not know how my father knew this, but he was certainly correct, for young Heatley was even then working with Howard Florey at Oxford on the purification and production of penicillin, a work in which he played a crucial part, since he was wonderfully dexterous with his hands; it was said that he could split a sheet of paper lengthwise into two sheets of equal size. When penicillin eventually came into common use (it replaced the newly discovered "M & B," which was nearly as effective) people generally thought it very strange that a mould could cure infections; we often joked that we would use mouldy cheese instead.

During the war, many large houses were "requisitioned," as the phrase went, as our Saint Joseph's had been, and immediately opposite number 109 was one such house, an elegant Italianate dwelling with a garden leading down towards the River Deben. I do not know what military unit was stationed there, but I remember that on one occasion a dispatch-rider on a motor-bike furiously rode up to the entrance, and as he got off the machine it burst into flames. In those days there were buckets of sand (and "stirrup-pumps") handy everywhere, and the rider calmly smothered the flames with a well-aimed volley of sand. Seven years old, I slowly got to know the area round 109. Next door was Dr. Robb, a family doctor with two teenage sons. They were very kind to me, in particular giving me a fine French model sailing-ship. It had a romantic history, for its twin had been lost when it sailed irretrievably out to sea in the English Channel from some beach in France. I often sailed it in the Woodbridge yacht-pond down by the river, and so did some of our children (Ch. 11, pl. 14).

Close by was also my new school. In those days, children often did not go to the local primary school if their parents could help it, so for a term I went to a sort of dames' school, run by Miss Runnacles and Miss Ray. I was of course hopelessly shy and made no friends. At home much time was taken up by domestic duties, which partly involved keeping the coal-scuttles charged with the coal left in a pile by Mr. Tricker, unloaded from his cart and horse. I also chopped a great deal of kindling in the cellar/basement with an axe, then lighting the various fires in different rooms, using a large sheet of newspaper across the sides of the fireplace to make a strong draft. In retrospect, this does not seem to have been very prudent.

We all had to be quiet at number 109, because my maternal grandfather, who had been an official with the excise service (making sure, for instance, that the local breweries paid their tax-duty), was dying of some kidney disease. He had been an active local Freemason, whose splendid regalia I could admire in a bedroom cupboard and had also acted in the plays put on by the local troupes, the Seckford and the Connard Players. He loved to sing, and, like acting, that was a large part of social life before radio and television. Alas, he also loved to drink to excess.

After his death, my still active grandmother joined the Women's Land Army as warden of one of their hostels. Her hostel occupied the old rectory in Halesworth, Suffolk, where Almena saw to the housing of twenty or so young women, coming from different parts of the country. They went out daily to help neighboring farmers, and also helped to entertain the many US airmen at the local bomber base; some marriages came out of these encounters. The Halesworth rectory, which I sometimes visited as a ten-year-old, provided many good stories. One of them concerned a man who called round early one day. My grandmother, taking him for an urgently needed plumber, hurried him upstairs. After unblocking a lavatory or two, he politely asked Almena "now, could you think about sending me one or two girls tomorrow?" for he was a local farmer.

Almena had three children: my mother and two older brothers. One of them, Alec, pursued a conventional career. Having served with distinction in the Royal Naval Reserve, receiving the DSC for his work as captain of minesweepers, he spent the rest of his life as a country attorney at the village of Bourton-on-the-Water (as beautiful as it sounds) in Gloucestershire. The other, Jack, was a stormy petrel, though a very good uncle for me; we played a lot of cricket together, often calling in at pubs on the way to games. He lived near Woodbridge, with his second wife, Wiggly, and worked in various forms of real estate. Many years later, we learned that Wiggly was in fact the mother of the Cornwell boys, whom she had abandoned to run away with Jack (her husband, Ronnie, having been cruel to her). The younger Cornwell, David, eventually became famous as John Le Carré, writer of spy fiction, who has described his mother's departure with Jack – "a ginger-moustached realtor". It introduced for the brothers a period of great turmoil, out of which John partly fashioned his plots.

After a few months with my grandmother, my parents moved to another house, on the northern edge of town. This Burkitt Road house had been built between the wars, and even to my child's eye was clearly less solid than number 109. It did have fascinating neighbors, though. Immediately opposite was the Lemaire family, living in a house that once belonged to the miller, whose windmill lay at the bottom of their garden. The mill was then more or less ruinate, an exciting place for little boys; now it has been restored and is a historical monument (5). In a large house to the south was an elderly couple with echoes of Africa, where the husband, Mr. Dobree, had been governor of some part of Rhodesia, and was said to have been among the first to cross the Victoria Falls on the spectacular new railway bridge.

(5) Buttrum's Mill, looking a good deal tidier than it did in the 1950s.

There were other echoes of a wider world around us. Next to the Rhodesian governor lived Dr. James and his wife and daughter, Mary. Dr. James had been an eye-surgeon at a London hospital, and during the war, in his retirement, edited the *British Journal of Ophthalmology*. The James family often fed me tea, when he would talk about stamp-collecting and nourish my growing collection, as well as discussing many other things. Another echo came from the local manager of Barclay's Bank, who sometimes gave me stamps from Kenya (6), where no doubt he had some planter clients; shades of *The Flame-trees of Thika*.

In fact, the generosity of people all over Woodbridge now seems amazing. I knew at least four families who used to give me the run of the libraries that their children had left, usually when they went into the Forces; I particularly remember the house in New Street where I borrowed gorgeously-bound copies of the novels of G.A. Henty, a fierce imperialist. I eventually became addicted to the work of Arthur Ransome, whose books like *Swallows and Amazons* recounted the adventures of four children, mainly in sailing-dinghies. Their mother stayed at home and ran the family, as the father was often absent as a captain in the Royal Navy. Britain still had a very large navy, and those who served in it, at whatever level, enjoyed a social prestige that is now completely unimaginable. Nothing of the same admiration clung to the Army or even, at first, to the Royal Air Force, known as the "Brylcreem Boys".

(6) Stamp celebrating the Silver Jubilee, 1936, from the manager of Barclay's Bank about 1940.

Perhaps I also envied the kind of large and relatively prosperous family described by Arthur Ransome. Its attraction for me, I now realize, resembled the popularity of figures like Ian Fleming's James Bond, for young men who wish that they were lecherous and adventurous. In the same way, Harry Potter has proved irresistible for children in need of credible magic exploits, in which they could imaginatively participate.

Ransome, Bond and Potter achieved their huge popularity by drawing their readers into tales of a distant and not quite attainable life.

The Seckford Public Library, looking out on the graveyard of Saint Mary's church, was also a great resource, with its numerous well-worn leather-bound books by authors like Robert Louis Stevenson and Captain Maryatt. It was a snug place in winter, with its open fire, and the three Redstones, father and two daughters, made it a welcome haven. They were renowned local historians, and eventually let me work in their private study at the Library, with its collection of books on Suffolk. The Norman castles of Suffolk, like Orford Castle, had a fascination for me, and I remember submitting an article on them to an Ipswich magazine called *The East Anglian*, which must have been astonished to receive this early effort. Of course, they did not publish it.

A year or two later, perhaps in 1944, my parents moved to a larger house in the same neighborhood. "Chaddeslode" (odd name!) was a large square house set in a spacious garden, which my schoolmaster father was probably only able to afford because rents had been frozen for the duration of the war. In 1939 the house, like many others, had been prepared for a bombing attack, with a large bank of sandbags protecting the wall outside the stairs, under which I had a snug bed, and the windows covered with sticky paper. This arrangement was never seriously tested, though I do remember sleeping in my shelter, when I once heard a stick of bombs going down, each one a little louder; "1-2-3-4-5-6"; perhaps one of these bombs was the one which landed in the millpond by the river. It killed many of the fish, including a huge conger eel that I saw on the bank the next morning. My parents were quite fatalistic, and continued to sleep in their upstairs bedroom, even after they had sent me down to my shelter. The only thing which disturbed them was the "doodle-bug," a flying bomb which you could hear gently puttering along until the engine ran out of fuel and it crashed, with a huge explosion. Eventually, skilful pilots in fast fighter aircraft learned how to fly alongside these machines and cause them to crash by lifting one of their short stubby wings.

The other kind of war-preparation involved the digging of a large vegetable-garden at the bottom of the lawn. There we grew all kinds of food for the kitchen, and also kept a flock of chickens. Their eggs were welcome, and their cockerel used to have fierce fights with the sea-gulls, who came to eat the chickens' food. The house was typical of medium-sized English houses of the period. The only permanent heating came from a stove in the kitchen, which also warmed the water, stored in a large tank in the "airing-cupboard" where freshly-washed clothes were kept. The airing-cupboard was a great place to get warm and to read, for the bedrooms in particular were so cold that on occasion water left overnight on a bedside table might freeze. One curious feature was the set of bells in the kitchen, joined to four or five rooms so that a maid could be summoned. We never, of course, used these bells, which were survivals of a rapidly-passing social system. In the middle of the kitchen was a huge clothes-rack hanging from the ceiling; it could be used to dry clothes, if the weather were not fine enough to use the clothes-line in the garden. No question of electric clothes-dryers.

The house was in general self-sufficient. Gas and electricity were supplied, but there was no garbage-collection service, and all the waste was either burned in the kitchen stove or put on the compost heap. The milkman came each day, to leave his bottles of milk and collect the empties, and occasionally Mr. Tricker would come to deliver a load of "coke," which we burned in the kitchen stove. Very little was packaged and everything got re-used; I remember my astonishment when, in the late 1940s, my father acquired a machine for making coffee, using a paper filter. When the coffee was made, he took the filter and I expected him to wash it for further use. When he threw it away, I had my first lesson in the disposable economy that was now emerging.

We generally ate a great many vegetables, spiced up with small portions of meat. Chicken was a great treat, often for occasions like Christmas, and sometimes friends would leave one or two pheasants that they had shot, or perhaps killed more or less by accident in the road. Our food betrayed little foreign influence, except that on Sundays we often ate an English version of more or less Indian curry, served on a large plate in the middle of the table. Sometimes, too, my father would get a pig's head and make from it the most delicious brawn, perhaps a survival from his Belgian childhood, when the family occasionally ate other odd things like blackbirds. In some respects, his diet would now be regarded as reprehensible; he liked, when he could, to eat bacon for breakfast, pouring off the fat so that he could eat it on a slice of bread at the end of the afternoon, which came late for him. Taking a great deal of exercise, particularly as a referee on the school playing-fields, he nevertheless survived to the age of 84.

I remember the excitement with which I saw my father open the first bottle of French wine after the war. Its exotic label made a great effect, as did the beautiful labels on wooden boxes of Tunisian dates, which also began to come in after the war. Rationing of standard food persisted longer than people expected, lasting in some cases until 1954. I do not remember food coming in under the counter, so to speak. But there were some delicious anomalies, one being a wonderful tea-room that became famous immediately after the war for its cakes, made from some abundant source of sugar best left uninvestigated. Black market dealings were in the hands of "spivs," a word that has quite passed out of fashion, even if spivs have not.

(7) Kurt Grunseid and I about to set off on our bicycles from Seckford Street. His dress looks a good deal more practical than mine.

Once I could ride a bicycle, Woodbridge and its surroundings became my oyster. I made many expeditions with my best friend, Kurt Grunseid (7). He had come by himself from somewhere in Germany, perhaps with the Kindertransport that brought so many refugee children to England in the late 1930s; he had to leave his parents behind. His guardian was Miss Covernton, a kindly schools inspector who had a well-equipped workshop where Kurt and I made all kinds of things out of wood. I also often went riding with Roddy Rose, son of a major in the Argyll and Sutherland Highlanders, billeted in Woodbridge. Major Rose, who had escaped when his battalion was captured in Malaya, would set a bottle up at the end of his garden, and use this for target-practice with his revolver. The roads around Woodbridge were in general fairly safe, but the bypass, constructed in the 1930s, was perilous, as it allowed one lane of fast traffic in each direction, with little room for cyclists. We generally kept away from it, but on one occasion we were riding on the bypass when Roddy suddenly decided to make a right turn across the traffic. There was the most appalling noise of skidding behind us, and a large Humber staff car slewed across the road. Out sprang some senior army officer with a red hat; he seized Roddy and gave him a good cuffing before driving on. It was safer to stick to the country roads.

My other friends were mostly those with whom I practiced games: cricket, hockey and rugby. In the snobbish way of the times, these boys from town hardly ever came to see me at home. Our family was indeed in a sort of ambiguous situation; we were much too poor to belong to sailing clubs, or to eat in restaurants, or to stay in hotels, but my mother would have taken it amiss, if I had brought home children whose local accent did not please her. Indeed, she took offence at some of my school-friends for this reason. The only time that I remember my father speaking crossly to Maidie was when he told her that it was quite immaterial how people spoke, as long as they had sensible things to say; she could never accept this idea.

Class distinctions were thus omnipresent and tedious in the England of my youth. On the other hand, people in Woodbridge seem already to have been very accepting of gay people. There was one in the town who was a great sailor (he had sailed his yacht to help in the evacuation at Dunkirk in 1940) and a good writer, and it seems to me that he was generally accepted; people just took it for granted that he was "like that." There did seem to be an easy casual relationship between people of different classes, many of whom knew each other from having served in some branch of the armed forces. This also sometimes gave them a rapidity of reaction that now seems remarkable. Once I was walking in Ipswich, the local county town, with my friend Patricia and her father, surgeon-admiral Corey. Just by us, a car hit a cyclist. Quick as a flash, the admiral reacted. I was sent to stop the traffic, Patricia was sent to call an ambulance, and the admiral himself attended to the cyclist. I could not help thinking of this event many years later, when I was eating breakfast in New Orleans with my cousin, a trauma surgeon. Outside the coffee-shop, a van drove fast into a light-pole, and the driver sat dazed and bleeding. My cousin had the appropriate reaction; eating another mouthful of scrambled egg, he opined that somebody would soon call an ambulance.

People in Woodbridge also seemed to have an easy relationship with the police, who patrolled the town singly and on foot. It was later that the police station was moved to the periphery of the town, and the constables began patrolling in cars. I remember, when I had come on a visit to Woodbridge in 1970, seeing some vandals pulling down part of a historic barn near the station. I thought better than to confront them, for by then the possibility of speedy help from the police did not seem to me good. The police by then also tolerated a much greater degree of drunken behavior when the pubs shut.

Perhaps my image of social relations in Woodbridge is too idyllic. It was challenged when in about 1948 I worked on a farm for the summer, gathering the corn into "shooks" to dry before it was carried away on a cart. One of my companions was a burly laborer who had been a sergeant in the Commandos during the war. He was understandably bitter about being unable to find other employment than that of a day-laborer, and told me many things about the local farmers, some of whom I knew from their visits to my parents, that were not pleasant. All this came back to me when eventually I read Ronald Blythe's *Akenfield*, which paints a bleak but convincing picture of the hard life of the rural laboring class in pre-war Suffolk.

During the war, there were airfields all round Woodbridge. The oldest one was at Martlesham Heath, which had played its part in the Battle of Britain (as part of 11 Group), when famous pilots like Douglas Bader and "Johnnie Johnson" had flown from there. Later it became home to one of the "Eagle" squadrons of volunteers from the United States, and you could see their Spitfires lined up along the perimeter as you took the bus into Ipswich; there is a memorial to them, buried in the commercial estate that the airfield has become. Later still, Martlesham housed a variety of experimental units, including one which flew a tailless aircraft that we called "the pterodactyl" as it swooped above us. The main road to Felixstowe crossed the chief runway at Martlesham, where you were often halted while some aircraft landed or took off.

Across the river from Woodbridge was the huge runway (nearly two miles long) at Sutton Heath, eventually known as RAF Woodbridge. This runway had been conceived to enable damaged aircraft returning from raids in Europe to make some sort of landing; as well as being very long it was also very broad. We would relatively often (when the wind was in the east) see four-engined bombers, with at least one of the engines out of action, fly low over Woodbridge on their way to Sutton Heath.

This airfield also had an amazing flare-path, for use in misty weather. It consisted of many fiery petrol braziers alongside the runway, and when it was in use the whole eastern horizon turned red. Sutton Heath enabled many damaged aircraft to land more or less safely. But one day, I remember, a four-engined American bomber (no doubt a Flying Fortress or a Liberator) had trouble with its approach. It would settle down for a landing, and then suddenly rear up. After one such manoeuvre, my father and I saw several parachutes emerge, before the aircraft plunged into the ground.

Adjacent to RAF Woodbridge was RAF Bentwaters, constructed a little later. It was a conventional airfield, notable during the latter stages of the war because it housed squadrons of fighter-bomber Typhoons, which did such fearful damage to the German armored forces in Normandy in 1944 (8).

(8) Drawing of a Hawker Typhoon, of the kind based at Bentwaters. It proved deadly in attacks on ground targets.

They had much noisier piston-engines (Napier Sabres) than the silky-smooth Rolls-Royce Merlins of the Spitfires at Martlesham, and they could easily be heard in Woodbridge, four miles away, as they warmed up. After the war, these two airfields were assigned to the United States Air Force, whose members thus became a long-lasting presence in the town of Woodbridge. My mother used to be much offended by some of the wives, who went shopping in Woodbridge with their hair piled in spectacular mounds of curlers. On the other hand, she greatly enjoyed playing bridge (at which she was very skilful) at the officers' club in Bentwaters, and my father liked teaching courses sponsored by the University of Maryland to the base airmen. Many of his pupils were those then known as "colored boys," and he felt a great affinity for some of them. My young brother also befriended a pair of young USAAF airmen who lived close to us in the 1950s; alas they were both, pilot and navigator, killed when their Thunderjet lost its engine on takeoff from Bentwaters.

During the War, the American Eighth Air Force also had many hastily-prepared bomber airfields in Suffolk. The nearest to Woodbridge was at Debach. I first became aware of it when, on a school walk, our way was suddenly impeded by a new barrier, behind which was an enormous silver aircraft; we had radically to change our route. It was no doubt the airmen from Debach who once rented the School's main assembly hall for Halloween, perhaps in 1944. When we used the hall for assembly the following day, there were witches in the rafters, the wooden floor was soaked, and the smell of beer was overpowering. One year, the USAAF sent us a runner to take an honorary part in Sports Day. He must have been some famous miler, whose effortless speed and acceleration left us astonished.

Debach was for a time the base from which the USAAF sent unmanned "drone" aircraft to attack particularly important targets, and it was while piloting one of these drones (from which he would eventually have parachuted) that President Kennedy's older brother was killed, when the aircraft, having received a rogue radio signal, blew up into many pieces over Blythburgh, near Southwold. At this time, too, my future brother-in-law, Bill Dalziel, was flying from a local base as belly-gunner in a B-17 bomber; he miraculously survived nearly thirty missions over some densely-defended German cities. Now my brother walks his dogs on that barely distinguishable airfield.

On the coast at the mouth of the River Deben was RAF Bawdsey, which in the 1930s had been the site of experiments that led to the construction of the chain of radar stations that played so crucial a role in the Battle of Britain. It was also the site of one of this chain, with its four tall towers and four shorter ones (9).

(9) The eight radar towers at Bawdsey, seen from the River Deben about 1945. The tall ones were for transmitting radio pulses, and the smaller ones for receiving them; a network of such tower-groups covered southeastern England.

I do not remember that in Woodbridge we ever really knew what purpose these towers served, as "radar" was for many years a closely-guarded secret, whose very name was shrouded in mystery. To be so close to so important an installation, and yet to know very little about it, has sometimes made me wonder if those Germans who claimed to know little about nearby concentration camps were not perhaps telling the truth. Bawdsey had a fine pebbly beach, on which the RAF had posted "Mines: danger." My mother, though, contended that some friends in the WRAF (Women's Royal Air Force), radar operators at Bawdsey, had assured her that these notices were just intended to keep the beach private, and so we often picnicked there in solitude and peace.

In general, my parents' generation took risks that we would now find excessive. On the Isle of Wight, for instance, the boys often roamed the high chalk cliffs by the sea, looking for sea-birds' eggs, and in calm weather they rowed far out to sea, even on occasion rounding the Needles at the western tip of the Island. It was also said that Julia, their mother, had rowed across the Solent to Hampshire, "keeping the bows pointed into the larger waves," but this is hard to believe.

Just north of Bawdsey was Shingle Street, a long stretch of open flat coast, where it was thought that German spies could easily land. For years there were rumours of such landings, which have never been verified. As a member of the Home Guard, my father spent many nights patrolling these beaches. After that, he would teach all day at Woodbridge School; small wonder that by 1945 he was at the beginning of a complete nervous breakdown. It was eventually cured thanks to a long spell in Saint Bartholomew's Hospital in London, and treatment with a variety of new drugs from the United States; his life was in effect thus saved, when he became an early beneficiary of the newly-established National Health Service.

The most spectacular single event of the war was no doubt the time when huge numbers of aircraft, many towing gliders, passed over Woodbridge on their way to the ill-fated parachute drop at Arnhem in 1944. This attempt to capture "a bridge too far," while ignoring intelligence reports suggesting that it was far too risky, ended in disaster. Like Dunkirk, this disaster became part of folklore, and after the war many people knew and respected the two fishmonger brothers in town who had fought there with the British airborne troops, and yet had escaped, just as they respected Deben yachtsmen who had sailed to France to help in the evacuation at Dunkirk in 1940.

The main road through the town, the "Thoroughfare," long retained its character. It had (and has) wonderful curves, which set off the great variety of buildings alongside the street to great advantage. Many of these buildings are shops, sometimes dating back to the seventeenth century. In the 1940s, housewives still congregated there to do their shopping in a number of specialized shops - the baker, the butcher, the fishmonger, the greengrocer and so on - and then take a cup of coffee with their friends, often arriving on bicycles equipped with huge baskets in front for their purchases. There were as yet no plastic bags, so people generally put vegetables directly into the baskets.

A smithy still survived on one of the lanes leading down to the river, and little boys could hang over his half-door, watching the molten metal being beaten out into horseshoes and other objects. The Thoroughfare still carried traffic in both directions, but it was dangerously narrow. I once saw an incident in which a British Army three-ton truck and an American GM truck of the same size, going in opposite directions, tried to pass in the middle of Woodbridge and, each miscalculating the width of the other, and neither wishing to give way, became firmly wedged in the middle of the road.

Eventually, all this changed. The Thoroughfare became a one-way street (and later was pedestrianized) and supermarket-type shops replaced most of the small, specialized ones. People still sometimes met their friends for coffee after shopping, but more and more women worked outside the home, and more and more of them came shopping in their cars, for which special parks began to be built. The influence of distant marketers began to be felt in many ways; local enterprises had less autonomy, and some changed their names. "Banks", for instance, now sometimes called themselves "Financial Centres," and plant-nurseries became "Garden Centres." Sometimes these changes led to problems. I remember that after I had been away from Woodbridge for some years, Barclay's Financial Centre sent me a curt letter (probably from the Midlands) saying that my account was too trifling for them to retain. It was indeed trifling, but, indignant, I told their representative that my family had banked at his bank in Woodbridge for seventy years, and that I declined to be rejected. Amazingly this rather historical argument was accepted, no doubt on the advice of some distant "Public Relations Consultant."

3

A Schoolboy at Woodbridge School 1941-1953

In the summer of 1941, I left the Runnacles-Ray school and was accepted into the lowest class at Woodbridge School. This local school had been founded in 1662, and after a flourishing eighteenth century had rather declined in the nineteenth and early twentieth centuries. The school relied in part on the Elizabethan benefaction known as the "Seckford Foundation," founded by a Tudor master of requests. This foundation became very prosperous towards the end of the twentieth century, and the school enjoyed part of this prosperity, increasing in both size and reputation; it now numbers nearly one thousand pupils, many from overseas.

By 1941 my father taught there (Mathematics, French and Latin), but I was never assigned to any of his classes. Our first classroom had been part of a chemistry laboratory; it was handy for the air-raid shelters which had been dug under a nearby grove of live-oaks (where they may yet be, under the ground). During imaginary air-raids, we would dash into these shelters.

In general, boys at Woodbridge School (there were as yet no girls) seem to have been a good deal wilder than they have become. From time to time the cry "Fight" would go up, as in *Tom Brown's Schooldays*, and we would form a ring around the combatants, until we were dispersed by the senior boys known as "prefects." Our favorite occupation during breaks in the school day was to play "hare and hounds" all round the school grounds. One of us was the hare, who had ten seconds' grace before the hounds set out after him. Sometimes he could survive until the bell called everybody back; if caught before that, he would be ceremonially tossed into one of the many gorse-bushes. Physical punishment was habitual, and I remember being caned by the headmaster, Canon Dudley Symon, for some breaking of the rules. Perhaps this was an astute move, to show that there was to be no favoritism.

For five years, I worked uneventfully up the classes. When I reached the age of twelve, a decision had to be made; should I remain at Woodbridge or try for a scholarship at Downside Abbey (my two uncles were Benedictines). Eventually, a compromise was reached; I would stay at Woodbridge, but now as a boarder in Marryott House (1). This was a huge stroke of luck, because the housemaster for Marryott was Desmond Proctor-Robinson, a descendant of the English Protestant ascendancy of Ireland trained (as were many of the masters) at Oxford University. "PR," a very confirmed bachelor, was a genius at drawing out his charges' talent. If they were sportsmen, he encouraged that. If they hoped to go into the Services, he encouraged that. If somebody was a little shy,

(1) Marryott House about 1960. It had been built in the mid-nineteenth century, in a sixteenth-century style.

PR would subtly draw him into some school play, to help him to express himself. Without a family of his own, PR made us feel that we were all his children.

In the English system of those days, pupils concentrated early on to enter either the arts stream or the natural sciences stream. I was stronger in the arts, and so studied History, French, English and Latin. But I have always regretted that I thus missed the amazing discoveries that had recently been made in unravelling the secrets of the atom, and knew nothing of the experiments in crystallography that were leading to an understanding of DNA, with the comprehension of the double helix. Indeed, in those days the natural sciences were thought to be the proper province only of "boffins." My German friend Kurt Grunseid was an exemplary boffin, who was too short-sighted to play the ball-games that we greatly prized; he eventually disappeared into the Atomic Energy Authority's station at Harwell.

French, English and Latin were taught in basically the same way; you absorbed the language by close study of two or three texts. In French, the one that I remember best was Molière's *Le Misanthrope*, which still seems to me the very model of what a play should be; it raises acutely some moral problems, without at any stage diminishing the dramatic tension. We also read widely in French poetry, from the sixteenth century onwards. Much of it was beyond the emotional range of English adolescents. But many verses by the leading Romantic poet Lamartine became my lifelong companions; who could resist:

O temps, suspends ton vol, et vous, heures propices,

Suspendez votre cours; laissez-nous savorer les rapides délices

Des plus beaux de nos jours?

[O time, delay your flight, and you, happy hours, hold back your passing; let us savor the fleeting delights of our happiest days...]

In those days, French Government Railways produced astonishingly beautiful posters, and I was entirely seduced by the images of Chenonceaux,

Mont Saint Michel, Chartres and the rest, which adorned our walls in Marryott House. Each year a French boy would come to help us with our accent. In 1947 this was Yves Bordeaux-Montrieux, from Paris and Burgundy. He seemed quite inept at lighting the fire in his study, and so some friends and I would do that for him. When he went back home at Christmas, he invited me to go with him. Crossing from Harwich to Antwerp, we spent a night in the medieval city of Bruges, and ever since then I have been under the spell of its painters: the Van Eycks, Hans Memling and the rest. We then went to stay in Bruxelles with Yves's sister, in an elegant flat near the Parc du Cinquantenaire (commemorating Belgium's less than admirable years in the Congo). Her first husband, a soldier, had been killed in 1940, and she had crafted a wonderful children's book in his memory, drawing on the legend of the heroic defence of the pass of Roncesvalles against the Moors in 778. Her second husband was a diplomat, who would rise high in the French Foreign Service, so that they naturally lived in some state. I was particularly struck by the great range of food that they ate, including things like tripe, horse-meat, artichokes and asparagus.

After Bruxelles we went on to Paris, where Yves's parents lived in an ancient house on the Left Bank (Rue de Grenelle). For Christmas itself, we went in a Citroën that ran on a wood fire (mounted on the rear bumper) to his family château in Burgundy (2).

(2) Photo of the *château* at Talmay in Burgundy, where I spent the Christmas of 1947.

This was an amazing experience; you could see the snow-capped peak of Mont Blanc from the top of the medieval tower, and the house itself still seemed rather down-at-heel from the war. Yves's mother was mayor of the village of Talmay, and I once went with her to a village meeting. The smell of garlic was overpowering, and I remember being astonished by the size of the villagers, among whom I felt like Gulliver, taller than most of them by a foot or so. Yves's father was a scholar much interested in early modern numerology, and in the music of the spheres. Indeed, he wrote a huge book on this theme, presenting a most elegant copy of it to the Pope.

(3) With John Proctor in France. We seem as usual
to be eating bread and cheese.

Later, when I was sixteen, I went with my friend John Proctor on our bicycles for a great two-week sweep through northeastern France (3). In those days, the locals were astonishingly kind to young English people. We never ate in the corner of a field without a chorus of "bon appétit" from passers-by, and twice, soaked to the skin in fierce rain-storms, we were rescued by sympathetic locals, spending one night in a warm laundry in Calais while our clothes dried, and another in the mayor's office of a little town in the Loire valley. We kept in touch with our parents by sending postcards every other day, an arrangement that now seems astonishingly casual. The northeastern parts of France still seemed to be suffering from the losses of the First World War; there were great numbers of black-clothed women at work everywhere, on the roads and in the fields. Often we slept in barns, and once we went to a youth hostel, which we shared with some German boys, fellow-cyclists. They were very cheerful and remarkably robust; I realize now that their parents must have been well placed in the Nazi regime.

English was taught in much the same way as French, with *Twelfth Night* and *Richard II* as the texts. Better, though, I picked up in a secondhand shop in Southwold a delightful india-paper copy of *The Oxford Book of English Verse*, and this has proved a lifelong companion. How could anybody not be entranced and bewitched by poems like Robert Herrick's (1591-1674) "Delight in Disorder?" It ends like this:

"A winning wave, deserving note, in the tempestuous petticoat;

A careless shoestring, in whose tie, I see a wild civility;

Do more bewitch me than when art is too precise in every part".

The combination of unexpected juxtaposed words with a very novel theme still seems to me irresistible; I have never appreciated the lugubrious ditties of the Philip Larkins.

For Latin, too, we had set texts: Caesar's *Gallic Wars* and Virgil's *Fourth Georgics*. Reading these, one could understand how a deep knowledge of this literature could bring together a whole culture with shared archetypes. Re-reading the *Fourth Georgics*, I have been dismayed to find how often I now have recourse to the English translation. But I also recalled how firmly some images had embedded themselves; how often have I not felt, in the summer under my arbor in Illinois, that I was one with the "old man of Tarentum, who took his ease under the high Oebelian vine?" It surely was easier for people in politics to reach an understanding, if most of their opponents had read the same texts and could at least appreciate common references to classical examples both of probity and of corruption.

History was a different matter. Students did not try to master the outline of, say, English or Latin literature. But "history" consisted essentially of learning the outline of some period of history, say Europe between 1485 and 1815. It thus lacked the immediacy that existed in the other subjects, where students came at once up against the actual texts in question. History needed hard grinding before its point became apparent. I remember when this was first revealed to me; in a university entrance-exam I answered a question about the social and economic effects of the war of 1815. All around, I could see similar effects after 1945, and was able to incorporate these into what seems to have been a successful answer. Once the background had been mastered, life itself was full of examples; I had learned by rote that English agriculture was ruined in the nineteenth century by foreign competition, but once I saw the prairies of North America and their vast and productive fields, it was obvious that no Victorian farmers would have been able to rival this bounty. "Only connect." The West Indies later proved to be a region where the past pressed in on the present with particular urgency.

A central part of whiggish English history was the long opposition to the Catholic powers of Spain and France. At Woodbridge in the 1940s, a young Catholic felt ill at ease. I remember once our geography teacher, an Anglican parson, telling us that Catholics were strange people because they listened to their service, oddly called a "Mass," with their backs to the altar (he was thinking of the reversible *prie-Dieux* in many French churches). I feebly protested that this was not so but was overruled. Our church in Woodbridge was an uninspiring structure that had formerly been a billiard-hall and gave no hint to me of the existence of a universal church ("securus judicat orbis terrarum"; she rules the world safely). But I do remember two intimations of this wider existence. One Christmas night, probably in 1944, the blackout was gloriously broken from the Catholic church, within which a party of German prisoners-of-war (no doubt very happy not to be on the Russian front or under the Atlantic Ocean) was loudly and harmoniously singing "Stille Nacht." Again, when we eventually went to camp with the army cadets, I would sometimes join the contingent from Ampleforth College, whose Benedictine chaplain celebrated the familiar Mass on the bonnet of a jeep, thus giving another hint of the church's adaptability and universality. Of course, once I crossed the Channel, a whole new Catholic world was revealed, even if it was at that very time in the process of melting away in many places.

Before joining the cadet force, though, I had joined the Scouts. They were led by Mr. Johnson, who also taught woodworking in the carpentry shop alongside Bredfield Road. He was a veteran Scout leader, who had just come back from Malta, where he had been a gunner during the German bombardment of the island; he had also learned to swim like a fish there, a relatively uncommon accomplishment in England in those days. The Scouts made great use of the classic *Scouting for Boys*, written by their founder, Sir Robert Baden-Powell (4). At one time I knew this work almost by heart and tried to follow its precepts. Some were a little absurd, like the injunction to ward off thirst in a hot country by sucking a small stone (though this has always worked for me).

'A trained scout will see little signs and tracks, he puts them together in his mind and quickly reads a meaning from them such as an untrained man would never arrive at.'

(4) The back cover of *Scouting for Boys*. Although Baden-Powell has sometimes been portrayed as an unthinking imperialist, he in fact had a great sympathy and admiration for a variety of indigenous peoples.

One section of the book described the use of a trek-cart, for Baden-Powell was strongly influenced by his experiences in the Boer War in South Africa ("trek" was a very Afrikaner word). We had one of these trek-carts stored in the area below the wood-working shop. It consisted of two large wheels each side of a large platform which had four shafts, two at each end. When we wanted to go camping, we loaded the cart up with our camping and personal equipment, and then, pulling the cart with a couple of Scouts on each of the shafts, made our way down to the railway station. There we loaded the cart into the goods-wagon, travelled as close to the camp-site as we could, and then unloaded it and made our way to the site. Of course, the procedure was reversed for our return, and this seems to have been a very satisfactory form of group travel (5). Once, when we were camping on the Norfolk Broads, I gave Mr. Johnson a bad fright, falling ill with a temperature and a fierce headache. In those days, we were all mortally afraid of contracting polio, before the days of the Salk vaccine; luckily my malady passed off after a day or two.

(5) A Scout trek-cart, as shown on a cigarette-card of about 1930.

We once went to camp at Gilwell Park, the very home of scouting in England. I mostly remember the extreme rigor with which our camp-sites were inspected, no doubt a legacy of Baden-Powell's experience with disease caused by sloppy housekeeping in South Africa, during the Boer War. Scouts were, of course, expected to be cheerful and modest people, not at all inclined to push themselves forward. It was rather a shock, in later life, to read of the energy with which Mrs. Baden-Powell pushed her soldier-sons' cases with generals and politicians over fashionable London dinner-parties; this was just another encounter with reality.

In general, nobody ever encouraged us in the belief, as has become the fashion in the United States, that if we worked hard enough anything was possible – even becoming prime minister, for instance. Our ambitions were much more modest, perhaps exemplified in the Winchester College and scriptural notion of becoming the "good and faithful servant." This did not encourage what George Bush the First called "the vision thing," which he correctly thought himself to lack, even though he had many other admirable qualities. But it did encourage the skill of making the most of whatever resources you had and discouraged self-promotion. We rather agreed with Dr. Johnson that "there is a reciprocal pleasure in governing and being governed."

Eventually, it made sense to leave the Scouts and join the Combined Cadet Force, for this was obviously a good training for the National Service to which we were mostly bound. The most remarkable figure in the CCF was Sergeant-Major Morgan, who had served with the Suffolk Regiment in Europe from Normandy into Germany, winning the Military Medal for gallantry in action. He had a fierce Irish accent, and many useful aphorisms. I best remember "what the eye don't see, the heart don't grieve over;" this has served me well for many years. The CCF had a band, in which I played a kettle-drum, very badly. Sometimes we led parades, and once a year paraded in front of the War Memorial by the chapel, with the names of Old Woodbridgians who had fallen in both World Wars. On these cold November mornings, one could not help wondering whose names would appear there next. But in the event, none of us did, being part of a lucky generation. Our only casualties came from those who had joined the RAF as pilots. I particularly remember Tom Frewer, who flew into a tree on a night flight, and Nicholas Parrott, whose Vampire stalled as he came in to land at Kai Tak, Hong Kong.

Sometimes we would hear of OWs who had performed deeds of daring; thus Tom Henson received the Military Cross for his leadership in the Royal Norfolk Regiment in Korea, as did Alan Horrex of the Suffolk Regiment for his work in the jungles of Malaya, where there was a communist-inspired insurrection. As a member of the CCF, you could during the holidays go on various courses. You were issued a railway voucher and travelled to places like Hythe and Colchester for courses in subjects like small-arms operation, section leading and physical education. It was a great exercise in self-reliance, even if the physical training instructors could not do much for spindly boys in ten days. Our parents sent us off across England into the clutches of the army in our early teens apparently without apprehension; this surely was a more trusting and unified society than it has become.

Once I went on such a course with my good friend Dudley Mathews, from British Guiana, who became a gynecological surgeon at a London hospital. Dudley was an excellent athlete and had early been trained by the Jesuits in Georgetown; he tried in vain to make me see the attraction of Milton's poetry. Dudley and I took against a rather ugly patch of ground by Marryott House, dug it over and planted a flower-bed; the authorities must have been very forbearing. We also played a lot of cricket together. I still remember the day that, aged eight or so, I realized that with care I could catch a high-hit cricket ball. Strangely, this faculty has never left me; I always had the feeling that if I could reach the right place, the ball would, as it were, home in on me, and so it generally did. As with many boys, cricket exercised a magical pull, encouraged by books like the elegant English batsman Walter Hammond's lyrical *Cricket my Destiny*, an account of his games each side of the 1939-1945 war, or Learie Constantine's *Cricket in the Sun*, an introduction to West Indian cricket.

Games played an important part in school life. On a games day, once a week, a list would be posted in the "quad" (a term from Oxford) of the day's teams for whatever sport was in season: cricket, rugby or hockey. It must have been a tedious job, in the days before computers, setting out teams for the whole lower school (perhaps 150 boys at that time), but this system meant that each of us played in at least one match a week. It must have been a torment for some, but it did mean that we all had at least a taste of these games. Eventually you might be chosen for one of the school teams, the Colts, the second eleven or even the first eleven, and then practice was more serious. On the whole, we did not encourage our parents to come and watch us at play; indeed, we felt that they brought bad luck, like women on a boat. Games seem to have been thought of as part of the process of coming-of-age, an individual development from which parents could, perhaps should, be excluded.

Each summer in the vacation, there would be a set of "nets" in which a professional coach would work on the cricket skills of the sons of prosperous local people: doctors, lawyers, shopkeepers and so forth. I remember one summer developing a gambit to join these gilded youths. I would first hang about where the balls were hit, gathering them up and throwing them back. Then, when there was a gap in the bowling in one of the nets, I would offer to bowl a little. Before long, the kindly Suffolk professional, Wally Duckham, would suggest that I also put my pads on and bat. He was a very good coach, whose own cricket career (for Worcestershire, I believe), had been sadly interrupted by his participation in the Second World War. Wally's favourite exhortation was "give it some stick, lad," and so we tried to. We did not wear protective gear like helmets but did not seem to suffer from the inevitable blows to the head and body.

At school, the outer world intruded from time to time. Once, when we were on a "nature walk" in the country near Hasketon, ambling along in a double crocodile, the word spread from mouth to mouth that HMS *Hood* had been sunk. Many of us knew of the *Hood,* a remarkably elegant battleship which unfortunately had inadequate protection above her powder-magazine (6). She had been sunk by the *Bismark,* herself then sunk after an epic chase in the Atlantic Ocean; we knew nothing of that.

(6) Drawing of HMS *Hood,* entering Portsmouth Harbour.

Once, in the course of a cricket match, a high-winged Lysander (an aeroplane much used for incursions into occupied Europe, for it took off or landed in very little space) flew low over the pavilion, and dropped a message for Captain Riddell, one of the veteran masters who had been wounded in the trenches of Flanders in 1914. On another occasion, the rumor spread that somebody had seen an aircraft with German markings on the runway at Woodbridge airfield, normally reserved for Allied aircraft in trouble. Many years later, I learned that this rumor must have referred to a Junkers 88 that had indeed become lost and landed in Suffolk by mistake, to the pilot's astonishment and dismay. In fact, it carried radar equipment that the English boffins were very glad to lay hands on (7).

(7) Photo of a Junkers 88 with British markings, probably the very one which mistakenly landed at Sutton Heath.

The last news from the outside world that I remember was the death of Gandhi, announced to a shocked school assembly. Of course, we had been rather astonished by the coming of Indian Independence in 1947, and the loss of that "jewel in the crown." We also knew of the mayhem that ensued. But the break-off of India and Pakistan was just the first of many such indications that the imperial fabric with which we had grown up was in the process of disintegrating, as country after country became independent from the British Empire in the 1960s. In the skies above, too, it was plain that British aircraft like the Meteor and Vampire were no match for the US aircraft now stationed at Bentwaters and Woodbridge. Indeed, I vividly remember an RAF Meteor flashing low over the playing-fields, with a USAF Sabre in hot pursuit; it was clear who was winning this friendly joust.

Aircraft were a great source of things to collect, specially from the dump of wrecked aircraft at the end of the Sutton Heath runway. I eventually had a small museum of these parts, arranged in a large cupboard at home, though I never succeeded in obtaining the coveted altimeter, a round instrument which told an aircraft's height above the ground. Kindly adults would sometimes pay to see this small museum, which also had fossils like sharks' teeth, ammonites and belemnites. It also contained corroded pieces of iron, which my friends and I had picked up from the inadequately-protected sixth-century ship that had been excavated in 1939 at Sutton Hoo, and that held a magnificent treasure. During the war, this site was sometimes used as a practice-pit by Bren-gun carriers, a form of small tracked personnel carrier. So perhaps our vandalism did not much matter by the side of this wholesale destruction; the whole site has now been taken in hand and is the site of a remarkable museum to commemorate an enigmatic royal burial on that little hill above the River Deben.

For a couple of years, I helped to edit *The Woodbridgian*, using a printing-method that had not changed for hundreds of years. After typing the various sections, you took them down to Fairweather's, a shop in Church Street that sold books and stationery and had a printery up some stairs at the back. You took your pages to the compositor there, who used individual metal letters of type, held in two "cases" (upper and lower), to form the text (in reverse) in an iron frame called a "form." A first printing from this form produced a set of "galleys" on which corrections could be entered, to prepare for the final printing. Gutenberg would have known his way about Fairweather's.

Eventually, the time came to take the entrance-examination to a university. After writing the preliminary papers at school, I first went on a very cold day in February 1952 to Oxford, where I was lodged at Magdalen College, in the superb eighteenth-century New Building overlooking a deer-park. The examiners at Magdalen were a formidable bunch, including figures like the famous and disputatious historian A.L. Rowse. They only offered me a place, so in December 1952 I went to Corpus Christi College in Cambridge, again lodging magnificently, this time in the New Court, built in the early nineteenth century. The Fellows of Corpus were more welcoming and offered me a scholarship which I delightedly accepted. I can still remember opening the telegram and realizing with amazement that I probably would not spend the rest of my life in Suffolk. Corpus would not accept home students until they had completed their National Service; mine began in March 1953.

Before leaving this chapter, I need to insert the image of a "letter" from the King that we all received at school in 1946 (8). Its sentiments may now seem a little artificial and cloying, but it did catch the period's sense of victory and even some sense of social unity; such a similar communication has long been inconceivable in England.

8th June, 1946

To-day, as we celebrate victory, I send this personal message to you and all other boys and girls at school. For you have shared in the hardships and dangers of a total war and you have shared no less in the triumph of the Allied Nations.

I know you will always feel proud to belong to a country which was capable of such supreme effort; proud, too, of parents and elder brothers and sisters who by their courage, endurance and enterprise brought victory. May these qualities be yours as you grow up and join in the common effort to establish among the nations of the world unity and peace.

George R.I.

(8) Message from George VI to schoolchildren, 1946.

4

Military Interval on Land 1953-1955

National Service in England seems to have been administered more or less without improper influence or favor. It was thought rather a poor show (as people would have said) to try to weasel out of it. One England cricketer, rejected on the grounds of his flat feet at the start of a brilliant international career, took years to live down this absurdity. Of course, we did not have the problem of our later American contemporaries, that we might be engaged in a detestable and unjust war. The campaign in Kenya was the most unworthy of our ventures, but this was a relatively small war, even if it brought grief to the father of Barack Obama. Needless to say, most of us did not reflect on why our service was necessary, or why, for instance, the Suez Canal remained an important "lifeline of empire," even though India was independent since 1947.

I had expected to be called up to the Suffolk Regiment, but to my surprise was told to report to the headquarters of the Royal Army Service Corps, in Aldershot. This was an unfashionable arm, devoted to supply and transport, and known to our rivals as "the galloping grocers." My fellow-recruits came from every conceivable part of the British Isles, and from a great variety of social strata. Many could barely read, and most had never used a toothbrush. On the whole we all mucked in (another phrase of the time) for six weeks of basic training, though some of us came to be known as "The F**ng Pox," or Potential Officer Cadets. This we achieved after passing the "wozbie," or War Office Selection Board. It had both mental and physical tests and involved each of us in turn leading our squad in improbable feats like crossing a stream using a variety of barrels and odds-and-ends of planking. All I remember of them is that we each had to swarm up a rope to a tree-branch; quite unused to that, my arms gave out at the top, and I crumpled down into a heap at the bottom. The supervising officer must have given me the benefit of the doubt; I had surely descended faster than most.

Potential National Service officers were trained at this time at Mons Barracks, in Aldershot. This was a sort of Sandhurst-lite, with ferocious sergeants from the Brigade of Guards, and an excellent cricket team, for whom I played. Indeed, I remember that there was a very timely game, against the Sussex Martlets, the day I should have taken the exam in military law. This has always remained a closed book to me, in spite of once having to defend in court (no doubt with extreme incompetence) a drunken soldier from Glasgow, who had run amok with a broken bottle. I surely should have failed that exam, even if I can still remember our fallback charge, so to speak: "conduct prejudicial to the maintenance of good order and military discipline." This would cover a multitude of sins. After three months it was pass-out time, with the elegant and well-born adjutant riding his horse off the parade ground after our final inspection.

Now we went to Buller Barracks, for specialized training in RASC functions. The winter was coming to an end, and our months at Buller (Sir Redvers Buller had been a remarkably incompetent general in the Boer War) were in some ways delightful. We would cruise about the countryside in northern Hampshire in our three-ton trucks, intimidating the inhabitants on those narrow lanes, avoiding imaginary ambushes, and supplying imaginary units with imaginary food and ammunition. Sometimes we would accompany our convoys on the motor-bikes which we had lately been taught how to ride, after a fashion; this gave our operations a delightfully military air.

(1) Passing-out parade at Buller Barracks, 20 November 1953.

The only really frightening part of our stay at Buller came when I had to "command" the passing-out parade. We had learned sword-drill, which gave one a very martial air, and I accompanied the inspecting general with my sword at the ready, as the image shows (1). The parade was quite complicated, with much marching and counter-marching to my loud commands. I often wondered what would happen if I either forgot what to say (things like "close order…. march!"), or even said the wrong thing. It was easy to imagine the chaos that would ensue, with the band playing at the wrong moment and my fellow-cadets marching off in the wrong direction. Some of my friends had indeed threatened to do just that as a prank, but luckily none of them came through with this threat.

Once commissioned, you were in the uneasy position of being saluted by all "inferior" ranks, including grizzled sergeant-majors who really were soldiers and could have been your father. In your turn, you had to salute all officers of the rank of major and above; it was a complicated hierarchy. This saluting would have been very tedious if we had habitually worn our uniforms for travel, but for that we had a kind of civilian dress which included a "porkpie" hat, handy for doffing if you met a lady. We had at this stage been offered a further course in "aircraft dispatching," or dropping supplies to British units from RAF transport aircraft. I have always slightly regretted not taking up that offer, which surely would have taken one to interesting places.

At some period during this training, we must have received inoculations appropriate to the area of our postings. All that I remember about that is that having been inoculated one Saturday, I began to feel very queasy when I was attending Mass the next day. This service was attended, for some reason, by a covey of senior officers, and I particularly did not want to vomit. So, I left the church, and took refuge in a little bush that was on an adjacent knoll. I have always wondered if my camouflage was sufficient, or if some kindly colonel simply decided to look the other way. Having "passed out" (as the phrase went) at the top of the intake, I was allowed to select my posting, and chose to go to Egypt, where Canal Army was some 80,000 soldiers strong. Since 1882 Egypt, nominally independent, had in fact been under British control, with her viceroys aiming to bring, as they claimed, "water and justice." However, Egypt had long been a semi-independent part of the Turkish Empire, and independence movements, taking the form of guerrilla warfare, were increasingly strong in the 1950s.

After a few days at Woodbridge, I was therefore told to report to the Underground station at Goodge Street in London; there we were taken off to the airport at Stansted in Essex, from which an Avro York flew us first to Malta, and then to RAF Fayid. The York was an interesting aircraft; a light conversion of the Avro Lancaster bomber (2).

(2) An Avro York of BOAC ("British Overseas Airways Corporation") coming in to land.

It was the first time that I had flown, and I remember the remarkable view of North Africa, where you could plainly see traces in the desert of the square fields left either by the Romans or, more recently, by the Italians. It occurred to me then that it would be interesting to look at a variety of countrysides from the air...

From Fayid I went to Ismailia, where some brigadier told me that I would be posted as assistant adjutant to the RASC School at Gebel Maryam (3). This was a unit which instructed drivers from other arms in the care of their vehicles and in desert navigation; my job involved routine administration (4). Occasionally newspaper pressure from England could be felt. On several occasions, journalists would report on the "scandal" that some soldiers in the Canal Zone had not fired a rifle in six months. Bad news for the assistant adjutant, who would spend the next week taking parties of drivers and cooks from many different regiments to the firing-range (5). Usually, we fired the standard 303 rifle, a development of the Lee-Enfield used at the turn of the century. Sometimes, though, we would use the Sten gun, a truly mortal weapon which often fired when you least expected it to do so (and often not, when you wanted it to do so), spraying the air with random bullets as we all sought cover. Our only serious small-arms weapon was the Bren gun, invented by the Czechs before the Second World War.

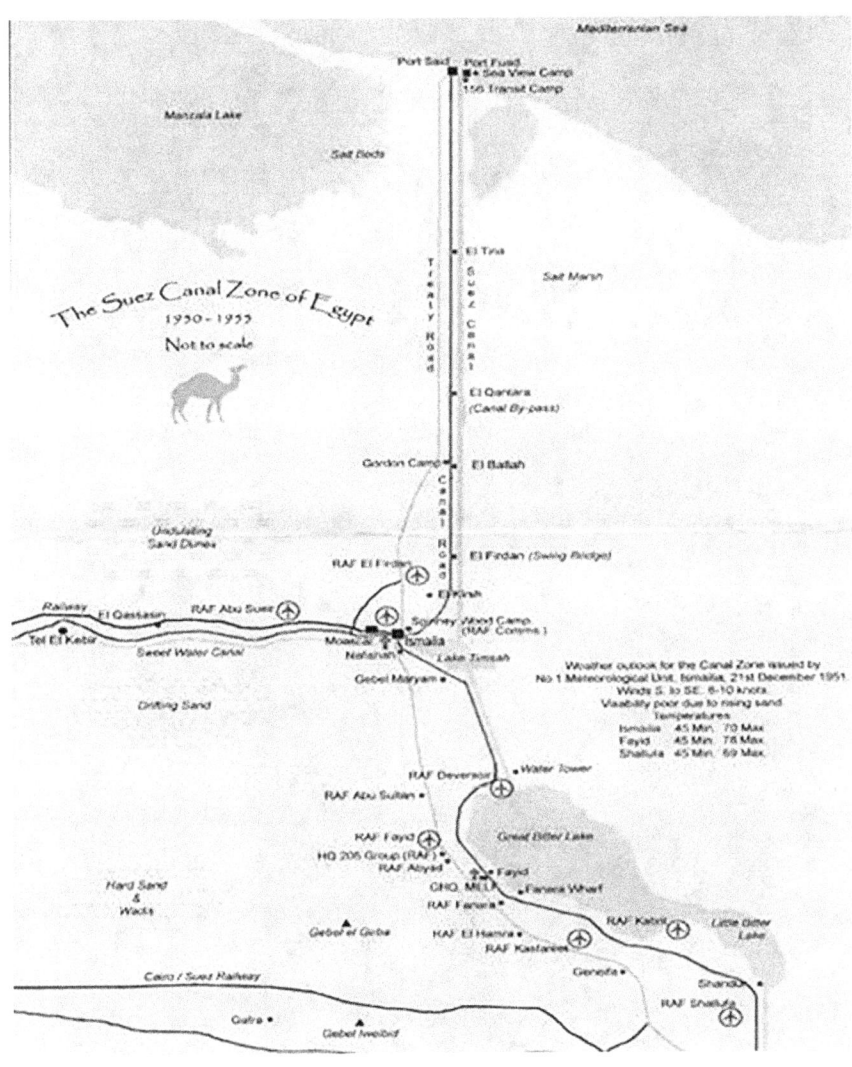

(3) The Suez Canal Zone of Egypt 1950-1955. Gebel Maryam lies just south of Lake Timsah, in the centre of the map; from Ismailia the main road ran west to Cairo, alongside the "Sweet Water Canal."

(4) Soldiers on duty outside Buller Camp, alongside the Canal.

(5) On the ranges, with Major Farmer and Sergeant Berry.

This was a semi-automatic weapon, rather like those which eventually came into service all over the world. My personal weapon was a 45 Webley revolver, a perfectly useless object in my hands; it required considerable skill and practice to be effective. As the phrase went, I surely could not have hit a barn door with it.

The base itself lay right by the Suez Canal, with a little river leading into the main waterway; the river's source lay to the west, where it lost itself in marshes. Among these marshes was the camp's water-filtration plant, which would prove a serious vulnerability. In the image from Google Earth (6), the present site of our camp is shown alongside the Canal. The main entrance, shown on plate 4, is clearly visible, leading to the parade-ground on which I organized many games of cricket and field-hockey.

(6) Google Earth image of Gebel Maryam today. The main square is visible, with what look like some British Army buildings alongside it. The lagoon leads into the Canal under a narrow cut, and the water-tower (plate 9) may still be seen.

Some little structures round the old parade-ground look like survivals from the days of Buller Camp, and the three large buildings seem to be part of some agricultural enterprise, supplied from the fertile surrounding fields. Across the Canal lay the vast desert in which Lawrence of Arabia had waged guerrilla warfare against the Turkish Empire.

In some ways Gebel Maryam was a delightful spot. The word meant "Hill of Mary," and tradition held that the Holy Family had passed this way on the flight into Egypt, though I have never been able to confirm or refute this theory. The Romans had had a camp there, and sometimes, when I took my motor-bike for a spin in the adjacent hills, Roman coins would shoot out from under the tires; I even picked one or two up, quite mindlessly. Apart from the bike, I usually travelled in a Bedford half-ton truck, on which Driver Buckley is working in the image (7).

(7) Driver Buckley is at work on the engine of our Bedford truck; my motorcycle is on the right, with the camp's perimeter-wire on the left.

(8) Outside my tent, about midday.

We lived in tents; mine is behind me in the photo (8). We ate like princes, for our unit shared the mess with the chief Middle East training unit of the Army Catering Corps, whose cooks would periodically offer us their superb passing-out confections. The waiters in the mess were recruited from the Sudan: tall and elegant men with deep scarifying tribal marks on their cheeks, wearing the usual long white gowns known as *galabiyas*.

Other locals notably included wonderful craftsmen who ran little shops by the square. The tailor could make a great variety of clothes, including in particular embroidered waistcoats, one of which I wore for many years. The cobbler's craft was even more magical. You could see him one morning, and he would draw round your feet in the sand. The next day he would sell you a pair of desert boots made to these measurements. Sometimes marketed in more recent times as "Wallabies," these wonderfully comfortable shoes were half-boots made of calfskin with thick rubber soles. They were sewn together, and would last for many years, even in wet northerly climes.

All the clothes from the camp were washed by the *dhobi-wallahs*, and all these adjacent personnel were paid monthly in a special parade by the assistant adjutant, using notes that eventually became almost unimaginably soiled.

Mention of *dhobi-wallahs* brings to mind other curious terms, often borrowed from parts further east. Some of the compound words were ingenious. Thus, to look at something was to "take a *shufti*," while the standard carrion-bird in those parts was a kite. A reconnaissance aircraft therefore became, in RAF lingo, a "*shufti-kite*." Milky tea, or *chai*, formed an important part of our diet. In the main cookhouse, we began eventually to hear complaints that the tea was too weak. Observation revealed that the local contractor had an arrangement with the cooks, whereby he collected the spent tea-leaves, dried them and sold them back to the cookhouse. Such ingenious frauds were common. They included the theft of wheels and tires from vehicles that had been imprudently parked, an operation that could be completed in an astonishingly short time, generally leaving the vehicle resting on large stones.

As sports officer, I was responsible not only for organizing games of cricket and field hockey against other units, but also for organizing intramural boxing matches. Occasionally officers would take part, though they never boxed against other ranks. Sometimes on these occasions the audience would show its sympathies; I particularly remember when one of my friends boxed against a Regular officer (from Sandhurst), and the soldiers left no doubt that their sympathies lay with their fellow conscript. Close by the parade-ground was a tall water-tower (still visible on the Google image), and from here we would observe ships coming down the Canal (9). Sometimes there were civilian ships, and sometimes troopships, the British going to Korea and the French to Indochina. I particularly remember the elegant *Pasteur*, which came through carrying French soldiers, some of whom would no doubt have been involved in the great French defeat at Dien Bien Phu, in May 1954.

(9) A liner coming down the Canal from the north; one of our
three-ton trucks is waiting to move onto the Canal Road.

The training which we offered mainly consisted of vehicle maintenance
and desert navigation. At that time, a great theory was adopted by the
British Army, following which we were to rely not on run-of-the-mill
vehicles like those turned out by Ford and Bedford, but on well-made and
extremely expensive trucks, sometimes with Rolls-Royce engines. The
theory was that these fine vehicles would not need the kind of improvised
attention with putty and tape that was traditional among our drivers.
Needless to say, this experiment was an expensive failure, when drivers
could not get at the engines for their home-made but ingenious and often
effective repairs.

Sometimes we went into the desert to the west for an exercise, with a
dozen or so three-ton trucks (10). Often, in those days, we met up with
camel caravans, on their way from the south to the markets around Cairo.
In theory, we navigated in that featureless expanse from "spot-height" to
"spot-height," these slight elevations being marked with oil on the sand.

Our chief navigation-instrument was the sun-compass, used effectively by units like the Long-Range Desert Group during the Second World War. In the photograph (11), I am directing the lead truck using the sun-compass mounted on the roof of the cab. It was easy enough to tell the driver which course to take, but we rarely ended up in the right place. This was yet another of those pre-electronic navigation-devices which required a skill that was beyond most operators.

(10) Seven trucks on exercise in the desert to the west of Gebel Maryam.

(11) Using the sun-compass from the hatch of a 3-ton Ford 4x4 truck.

Life at Gebel Maryam was not all beer and skittles. From time to time there would be shots from the adjacent marshland, and sometimes bullet-holes would appear in the roofs of our tents. Sometimes, too, we would find pamphlets like the one shown (12). This is a relatively crude example, but some were well contrived. One showed a British soldier looking in vain for his rifle. The legend below read: "You've got it/We want it. We get it/You've had it." The ambivalent nature of "you've had it" seems worthy of analysis by some postmodern linguist. There was also a pamphlet setting out rewards for killing British servicemen. I remember that the remuneration for killing a second lieutenant (like me) was greatly inferior to that offered for a sergeant-major, a true estimate of our relative importance.

(12) An Egyptian pamphlet, found alongside the perimeter wire. The soldier peeling potatoes is well observed, though the rock-breaker is less convincing.

It seems to me that I was in fact wonderfully lucky not to have attracted the attention of Egyptian malcontents. In particular, Pay-Sergeant Torrance (from Edinburgh) and I would almost weekly go on my motorbike into Ismailia (Sergeant Torrance riding pillion) along the Canal Road and through several villages, to collect pay for the soldiers and civilians in the Camp. Sometimes guerrillas would string wires across the road, thus decapitating several soldiers who were driving with their Landrovers' windscreens flat. Eventually most Landrovers were equipped with substantial shears above the engine, to cut such wires. It would have been remarkably easy to knock Sergeant Torrance and me off our machine, and of course to take the often-substantial amounts of money that we were carrying. Luckily nobody tried this trick; perhaps they imagined that I had better control of the machine than I did.

Sergeant Torrance was in fact very bold to ride pillion in this way. I seem to remember that we would quite often play tennis together on the courts by the Sergeants' Mess, though this surely was in violation of military convention at the time. In fact, I quite often visited the Sergeants' Mess, when parties of entertainers ("ENSA" parties, often including figures well known on the radio) came to the camp. The assistant adjutant was responsible for organizing their concerts, after which they were thought to feel more at home in the Sergeants' Mess. It seems to me that Sergeant Torrance also once sold me an excellent little German camera, a transaction that was also probably unconventional.

The only serious incident that troubled our calm existence occurred with the boat that carried shifts of engineers to look after the filtration plant, about a quarter of a mile away in the marshes. The boat carried one or two Royal Engineers ("sappers") and was guarded by one or two Royal Marines. One night, as it made its way along the narrow channel, it was ambushed by guerrillas firing from the reeds on the bank at close range. The Marines did their best to return fire, but they were using our standard World War One-type rifles, against their assailants' Kalashnikovs, and they were soon dead, as were the sappers. Our duty officer that night was a keen Regular officer, who on hearing the noise set out with the guard in hot pursuit. Of course, the guerrillas melted into the swamp, and there was nothing to do but to recover the riddled boat and the dead bodies. Our commanding officer told me to go the next day and examine the site. I duly took a boat and some men and went into the marshes. I had not had time to draw a serious weapon like a Bren gun, and remember thinking, as I sprang traditionally ashore with my useless revolver, "what a foolish way to go." But all was calm.

The dead soldiers were taken for burial by our doctor, Ralph Shulman, with whom I then shared a tent. He was a recently-graduated medical student from Glasgow, and came from a Jewish family there. In the Mess, I thus found myself in the position of having to defend the Jewish position in Palestine against some sharp criticism. I remember in particular a REME ("Royal Electrical and Mechanical Engineers") captain who had not long before served in Palestine with an infantry unit. These soldiers had among them a Jewish corporal who, my friend said, had betrayed their operational plans to the Jewish "terrorist" group against whom they were about to operate. If the story is true, his antagonism to Ralph and thus to me is understandable.

Ralph eventually had an opportunity to test his medical skills on me. One day I woke with a sharp pain in my chest; it got worse when one breathed deeply. Brandishing his stethoscope, and leafing over his medical encyclopedia, Ralph announced that I had "Q fever," or virus pneumonia, probably contracted from the sheep which roamed through our campground. We got into his ambulance (which my little unit had carefully maintained), and drove to the base hospital at Fayid, where his diagnosis was confirmed. There I might have perished, but the hospital, largely staffed by National Servicemen like me, luckily had received supplies of the newish antibiotic aureomycin, which was effective in curing the disease.

In fact, having returned to full duties too soon, I had a relapse some weeks later. On this occasion I remember feeling the day before a sensation of excessive good health, which George Eliot described as feeling "dangerously well." Back in the base hospital, I encountered a fierce nurse who remarked that patients with a recurrence of "Q fever" (the name comes from the sheep-rich state of Queensland) often contracted tuberculosis, and that I should surely be sent back to England. Luckily, I reflected that a nurse who was so unthinking was also probably ill-informed, and so it turned out. I returned to my duties, organizing ever more elaborate sports events and keeping my little park of vehicles in a high state of polish.

It must have been about now that two friends and I ventured to Cairo. This great city had often been out of bounds, due to what were euphemistically called "events," but now there was an interval of calm. Taking our out-of-bounds map (13), we drove to Cairo in a Landrover, equipped with a cutter. Curiously, I find in my diary for that year a visiting-card of "Sir Ralph Skrine Stevenson", "His Britannic Majesty's Ambassador Extraordinary" in Cairo. Did obscure officers from an unfashionable arm of the service have to present their cards to the Ambassador? It rather looks like it, yet another archaic survival. Of course, we were astonished by the great monuments, freely wandering by the pyramids and sphinx. I was particularly amazed by the skill of the workers in silver, brass, wood and leather in the *souk*, where indeed we must have presented a tempting target. Some of my friends took lessons in Arabic, which was a very sensible thing to do. But I found it very difficult to follow academic studies and found myself reading and re-reading books like Bryce's *Holy Roman Empire* without really coming to grips with them.

As well as reading, we entertained ourselves by listening to the Forces' radio. Apart from news sessions, there were the usual soldierly songs like the one beginning "roll me over/in the clover/roll me over, lay me down and do it again." Some of these songs were designed especially for us, like the one with the chorus "See the pyramids along the Nile? Just remember, darling, all the while/ you belong to me." Oddly, our radio often played the wonderfully lilting "Lilli Marlene." It had formerly been a favourite both of the Afrika Korps and the British Eighth Army, particularly in the version most langorously chanted by Marlene Dietrich.

My time in Egypt came to an end in May 1955. Before leaving, I went to the elegant French-designed headquarters of the Suez Canal Company in Ismailia, and tried to get employment for my batman, Ahmed. He was a remarkably efficient and friendly young man, and the only thing that he ever stole was my silver-mounted cane from Buller

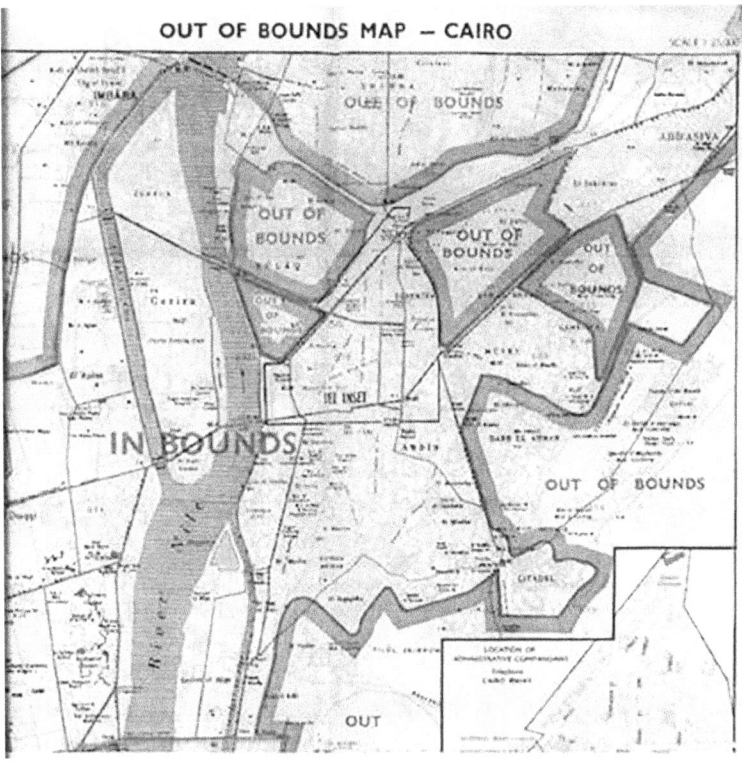

(13) The "Out of Bounds" map for Cairo that we took on our visit there.

Barracks (the "swagger-stick" given to the commander of the passing-out parade). I hope that it still survives on some Egyptian mantelpiece. Back in the Avro York at R.A.F. Fayid, we set off for England. Soon, alas, one of the four piston engines began to give trouble, and we had to land a little further west along the North African coast, at RAF El Adem. This was near Tobruk, and in that town I sent a cable to Suffolk, explaining our predicament. The pilot was a resourceful type, and soon lent a hand with the dismantling of the engine, and the installation of a new one, flown in from England. My friend Maurice King, the doctor who had succeeded Ralph Shulman (and later a major figure in tropical medicine, author of the widely-used *Medical Care in Developing Countries*) is standing by this work (14).

(14) Dr. Maurice King, dressed as elegantly as usual, by the work
going on to replace one of the engines on the Avro York.

El Adem was in those days still littered with the detritus of war, with rusting hulks of unidentifiable vehicles all over the place, from the fierce tank-battles between the Eighth Army and Rommel's Afrika Korps. Strangely, our time there marked a kind of turning in my intellectual life, towards the use of aerial imagery.

(15) Admiring the flight of Vampires that came to land at El Adem.

One day, a flight of six RAF Vampire aircraft came in to land (15). The De Havilland Vampire was a most elegant little aeroplane, with a single small jet engine and twin booms (chapter 5, plate 1). As I watched these six wraiths peel off and land, I thought to myself, "what am I doing in khaki, when I could be taking part in this lovely flying business?" It perhaps did not strike me then, but I had swiftly been bewitched by the possibilities of looking at lands and their peoples in a way that was impossible to the earth-bound, and this would eventually lead to a series of books examining "history from the air."

5

Military Interval in the Air, 1955-1958, and its sequel

Going up to Cambridge University in October 1955, my timing was good, for the University Air Squadron had just decided to begin training not only pilots but also navigators, and I joined this group. The Squadron, founded in 1925, had long brought together members of the University and leaders of the Royal Air Force; indeed, Air Marshal Tedder, second-in-command to General Eisenhower during the Normandy invasion in 1944, was a Cambridge graduate whose doctoral thesis concerned Samuel Pepys, the seventeenth-century diarist. Like its counterparts at Oxford and other British universities, the CUAS had provided a wealth of skilled aircrew during the Second World War, including some fighter-pilots during the Battle of Britain in 1940. Its regular staff were often rather intellectual people. When I enquired of the Commanding Officer if I could continue to serve out my time in the army, the wing commander replied that in his view "no man can serve two masters…" More prosaically, some other Squadron members remarked that they were always glad to welcome "brown jobs" who had seen the error of their ways.

The Squadron probably extended its activity into navigation in 1955 because it wished to profit by the presumed mathematical skills of Cambridge students. So we would go one evening a week to classroom activities, and more or less as often as we felt like it to Marshall's Airfield, on the outskirts of Cambridge, where we could practice our skills in a couple of Anson aircraft, navigating our way around England. In fact, the techniques which we learned were essentially those which had been rather unsuccessfully applied during the RAF bombing of Germany in the Second World War. It took a great deal of skill to use either "dead reckoning" or the complicated radar lattices known as "Loran" and "Gee," and only navigators like my friend Sam Conlon, an Australian mathematician from St. John's College, who eventually held the chair of mathematics at the University of Sydney, became really proficient at this discipline. For my part, it seems to me that I once landed in Jersey, while aiming for Guernsey; after all, they are both Channel Islands.

We were also taught some interesting adjacent skills. In order to fly in the De Havilland Vampire, we had to be trained in the ground version of the Martin-Baker ejector seat, which explosively shot you fifteen feet or so up in the air along a rail. We also practiced getting into a life-raft in the sea, from which you would then be plucked by a helicopter, an odd feeling. Best, though, for somebody who had never flown in other than piston-engined aircraft, was our flight in the Vampire (1). I then knew exactly what the great German wartime pilot Adolf Galland meant, when he wrote that flying in a small jet for the first time was "like riding on the back of an angel."

(1) RAF training-aircraft from the 1950s; a Gloster
Meteor (above) and a De Havilland Vampire.

Perhaps disappointed by the mathematical skills of students like me, the RAF soon closed down its navigation section, which meant that I could transfer to the pilots' group. They trained at that time on a recent little aircraft, introduced in 1950, known as a De Havilland Chipmunk (2). It sat on a rear wheel on the ground, which meant that when taxying one had to weave from side to side in order to see ahead, as in a Spitfire. Once in the air, though, this was a delicious little aerobatic aircraft, on which one could perform all the standard manoeuvres: loops, barrel rolls, stall turns, long sessions of inverted flight, which inadvertently enabled one to study the English countryside. I was eventually allowed to practice these manoeuvres in formation with my friend Ian Plimmer, who later joined the British Colonial Service (3). It was with Plimmer that I had my only narrow escape. Before making a manoeuvre, one would say on the radio something like" rolling right, rolling right, **now**." For some reason, before performing this manoeuvre I once said only "rolling right." I saw Ian's propeller flash a few feet past my tail-rudder; we both would have come to grief through my carelessness.

(2) De Havilland Chipmunk from Cambridge University Air Squadron.

Since the airfield was so close, we could fly virtually at will, and often went at night. It was a remarkable feeling to be floating over Cambridge on a clear winter's night. During the day, I thought of the air as a fluid, in which one manoeuvred rather as one swam underwater with a mask and flippers. But night-flying was a different feeling, particularly when landing; then it felt as if you were going to burrow beneath the ground (we used a large grassy area, without concrete runways). The RAF kept us firmly in our place; even though we might have 350 hours or so of flying, largely because of the yearly summer camps; we were never allowed to qualify for our "wings," or to rise above the lowly rank of "Acting Pilot Officer." Our aircraft were also given what seemed to me rather jocular call-signs; one summer we were "Primrose," and another "Dandelion." It was a curious feeling, to navigate across England and then call up a huge airfield like RAF Burtonwood in Lancashire (full of immense USAF transatlantic aircraft) for landing, using the call-sign "Primrose 6." As we rolled down their massive runway, we would learn that eight ambulances and ten fire-trucks were available, should we need them; a further element of fantasy.

(3) In dispersal at RAF Martlesham with Ian Plimmer, my flying partner. We are waiting to fly, wearing our life-jackets and with our parachutes at the ready, as well as a few textbooks.

The actual process of navigation was much more demanding than it has since become, with the universal use of some form of Global Positioning System. You would file a flight plan, and then mark it on a series of maps, which you kept attached to your knee, for easy reference. Getting lost was not likely if you were near some prominent object like the North Sea, but it could be quite easy to get disoriented over the complex and often undifferentiated English countryside. Of course, if the winds were strong, they could easily blow our little Chipmunks far away from their plotted course, and we always hoped that the forecast predicting clear weather, with nice fleecy clouds, in and out of which we could (illicitly) zoom and dog-fight, was correct. If the clouds came down or at night, we could always use radio instructions to navigate blind to our airfield, as I had qualified for an instrument rating (4).

(4) My white instrument pilot rating, July 1958.

I had at one time thought that after graduating from Cambridge I might try to join the Regular Air Force (we formed part of what was known as the "Royal Air Force Volunteer Reserve"), but things eventually took a quite different course, both personally and in a tactical sense. We had been training largely with a view one day to intercept the Russian bombers ("Bears") which could carry atomic weapons. But in the late 1950s this form of warfare became quite obsolete, when intercontinental ballistic missiles were developed. The old designations of "Fighter Command" and "Bomber Command" would soon fade away in the face of this new and terrifying reality, against which our emerging skills would have been useless. In fact, the Royal Air Force was entering a long period of numerical decline, which would have proved dispiriting to a career officer; as the phrase went, I soon would have been flying a golf club.

However, performing aerobatics above the English countryside gave one an unrivalled view of a great variety of earthworks, from neolithic mounds to recent fortifications. At this time, the University's Curator of Aerial Photography, Dr. Saint Joseph, was using the aircraft of the Squadron to make images of the English countryside, and I asked him if he could use any help in cataloguing the abundant material (then held in the former Corpus games-pavilion). Disappointingly, he said that he could not. After leaving the Squadron I therefore watched for an opportunity to apply the aerial view to developments in history. This opportunity came when we went in 1964 to Jamaica (chapter 9), an ideal country for aerial photography, with weather that was often fine, plenty of cane-fields for emergency landings and few other aircraft. Pat and I joined the local flying club and began taking our own photographs from its Cessna 150 (5)(6). In retrospect, this was not a very intelligent thing to do, for a young married couple with two small children at home in a strange country.

(5) Ready to fly the Cessna 150, from a field with elegant palm-trees.

(6) Pat checks the Cessna's oil.

The Institute of Jamaica (now the National Library of Jamaica) held a remarkable set of plans of estates from the early eighteenth century onwards, and we began photographing these estates and other sites from the Cessna. Of course, the results, shot out of the passenger's open window, often in conditions of some turbulence, were not remarkable, though they were improving. It was then that we made the acquaintance of Jack Tyndale-Biscoe. He was a professional Jamaican photographer, who after training as a flight-mechanic with Pan American, and qualifying as a pilot, operated his own aerial photography service out of the Norman Manley Kingston airport, then called "Palisadoes." Jack had a huge library of images of all kinds of site taken all over Jamaica, and it was a great delight to go and see him and his wife Marjorie, who organized the images, and select from them such views as seemed to throw light on the history of Jamaica, in conjunction with the material from the Institute of Jamaica.

The decline of the sugar estates after the abolition of slavery in 1833 meant that many of them had reverted to bush or were "ruinate" as the phrase goes. Nevertheless, using the early plans it was generally possible to identify the sites, and then to isolate such features as field-boundaries, roads, slave-quarters and so forth, often when these features could no longer be seen on the ground. I collected images and texts of the most interesting sites, and Jack and I published the first edition of our *Historic Jamaica from the Air* in 1969 by Caribbean Universities Press. I had myself drawn the maps and explanatory plans for this first edition, but when the second edition was published by Randle Publishers, at Kingston in 1997, we used more innovative maps by Tom Willcockson, and a good many color spreads. This made a handsome book which still sells modestly, mostly in Jamaica.

Since those early days the material at the Institute has also been fully exploited by Barry Higman, in his *Jamaica Surveyed* (Kingston, 1988 and 2001). Barry and I found that this material was ideal for teaching students in their final year, when they could offer interpretations of each kind of evidence in the light of the others. To this day, Jamaica probably remains the only place in which a systematic effort has been made to incorporate material of this kind in the teaching of history.

When I came to Chicago in 1980 to look after the Smith Center for the History of Cartography at The Newberry Library, we had an embarrassing problem. As the Director of Research and Education, Richard Brown, put it to me, "David, we have to do something about all this money." Feeling like some modern-day defence contractor, upon whom a grateful (and heavily lobbied) Congress is pressing funds, I wondered what to do. And then it occurred to me that flying was a fine way to consume lots of money, and that aerial analysis of the kind that we had undertaken in Jamaica might also work for Illinois. Friends put me in touch with Ernst Seinwill, a freelance aerial photographer who had worked for Chicago Aerial Survey, then in the process of going defunct (we recovered some of its reels of film for the Newberry).

Ernst had been a young member of the Luftwaffe, and he had the slightly unnerving habit of asking me, when I showed him the map of Illinois on which our potential sites had been marked, "Ach so; where is the first target?" We flew together many times, up and down Illinois. Of course, we could not even so be sure that we had the best images and lighting for every site, but after two years or so we had generated enough images for *Historic Illinois from the Air*. This book was greatly improved by the maps and other imagery supplied by Tom Willcockson, the Center's cartographer, and was published by The University of Chicago Press in 1990 (7).

(7) The dust-jacket of *Historic Illinois from the Air* (Chicago, 1990).

This time the book caught a sort of upswing in fashion; geographers in particular appreciated its use of different types of imagery to explain historical developments, and it was awarded several prizes, including the Jackson Prize of the American Geographical Association. Tom and I would have liked to follow it up with a book called "The Historic Great Lakes from the Air," in which we would have crossed the international boundary to draw out developments from the seventeenth century onwards, as well as dealing with ecological themes, but we could not find a publisher; this tempting theme has still not been tackled.

I had thought that this was the end of my ventures into aerial imagery, but when we went to Texas in 1995, my colleagues at the Department of History in the University of Texas at Arlington proposed that we collaborate on a work about Texas like the ones on Illinois and Jamaica. Our qualifications seemed ideal. Richard Francaviglia had published widely on the West, and in particular on its mining communities. Gerald Saxon was particularly well versed on the nineteenth- and twentieth-century history of the state, and I had been studying its history during its Spanish and French phases. Our aerial photographer was a former student, Jack Graves, whose work was superior to that of either of my two preceding books. The book, published by the University of Texas Press, was handsome, and received good reviews (8). Curiously, though, it did not achieve anything like the success of the Illinois book, being bought by fewer than half as many libraries as in Illinois, a smaller state. Perhaps the authors did not do the necessary legwork in the state; Richard and I had soon left the University, and Gerald was entirely consumed by his duties as Dean of Libraries. So our book sold modestly, eventually going out of print.

In general, the use of aerial photography to study human settlement does not seem to have been exploited as well as once seemed possible. There are many coffee-table books, with titles like "New York Then and Now," but few books which attempt to use aerial images, often alongside early maps, to offer a detailed explanation of the many material aspects of history for which these vehicles are so suitable. Even with the arrival of Google Earth, surely the supreme device for aerial imagery, its potential still seems to be unexploited; maybe in the age of sophisticated types of imagery (radar, infrared and so forth) the mere use of the parts of the spectrum available to human eyes has come to seem old hat.

(8) View of the state capitol in Austin, from *Historic Texas from the Air* (Austin, 2009).

6

Undergraduate at Cambridge 1955-1958

Cambridge University in 1955 had about twenty colleges, ranging in size from about 250 undergraduates to over 600 of them, and it was these often ancient institutions that formed the core of the University. Indeed, visitors who were used to other arrangements often complained that they could not see the university for the colleges. My college, Corpus Christi ("CCC"), was among the smallest, and had been founded in 1352 to make up for the losses of learned men as a result of the Black Death. One newspaper account described us as "pious and meritocratic;" its members were certainly not given to the kinds of excess so elegantly described by Evelyn Waugh in work like *Brideshead Revisited*. It lay in the heart of the city, with its three green lawns showing up on Google Earth at the intersection of King's Parade and Downing Street (1).

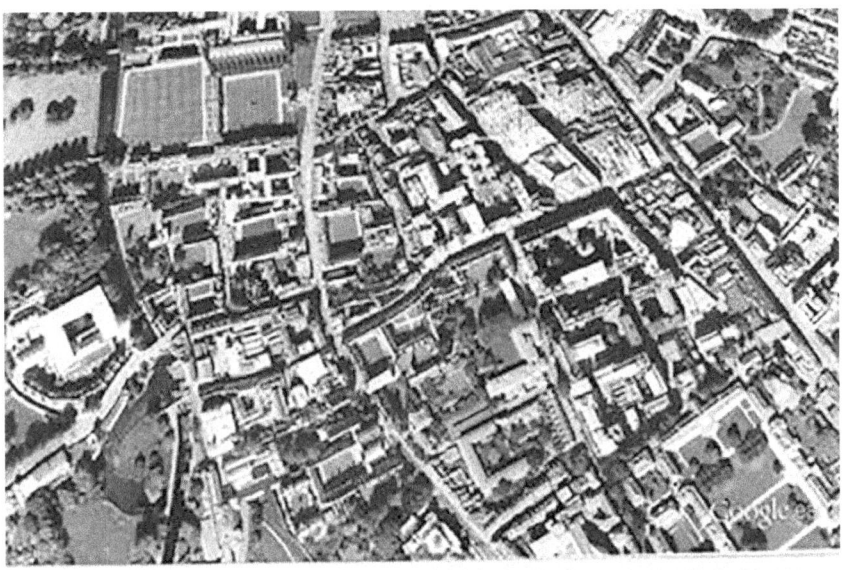

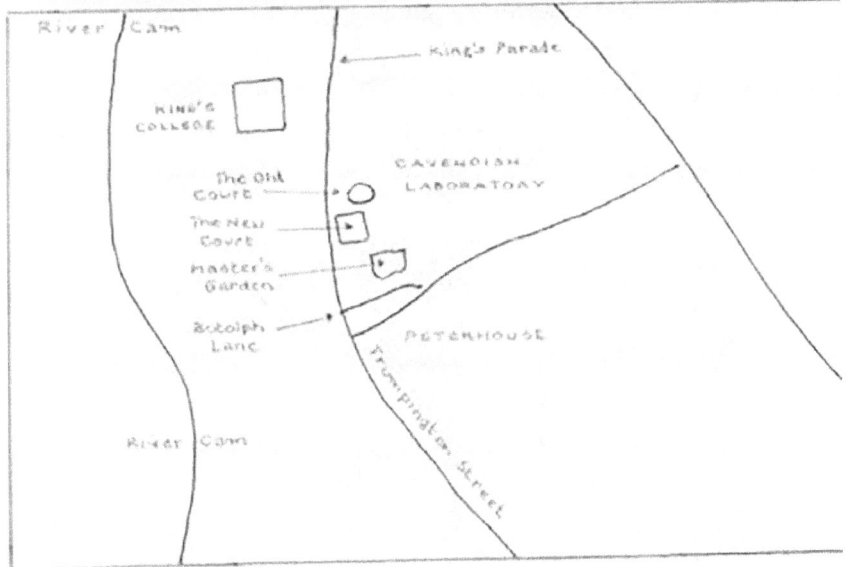

(1) Central Cambridge from Google Earth to show Corpus
Christi College (central large square).

Immediately to the east was the Cavendish Laboratory, where a revolution in the understanding of the physical world had been going on between about 1900 and 1940, leading eventually, alas, to the construction of atomic weapons, as well as to the peaceful use of atomic power. In the 1950s, its unimpressive buildings were the home of another revolution, when Francis Crick and James Watson were working out the structure of DNA, thus leading to an equally far-reaching new understanding of life itself. I knew nothing of this at the time, even though the laboratory where Crick and Watson worked was literally under my window.

When we arrived in the autumn of 1955, my group of undergraduates had nearly all come straight from the armed forces, where they had mostly served as very junior officers. Michael had spent his time over the Atlantic Ocean, looking for Soviet submarines from his naval aircraft. John had been a surveyor in Korea, aligning the fields of fire for artillery. James had served with the Black Watch in Germany, commanding an infantry platoon. Philip had been intelligence officer for his regiment in Malaya, assessing the movement of guerrillas in the jungle. The range of our experiences must have been comparable to that of students these days, during their invaluable "gap year" between school and university. Our sometimes gruelling experience surely gave us all a heightened appreciation of the apparently leisurely yet intellectually demanding life that was coming.

In one respect, we were less satisfactory material than modern students, for we had been cogs in a large machine that valued conformity and obedience, as well as efficiency. This made many of us over-conventional, as became clear over the years. Our contemporaries who had not been officers, but who had often been sergeants in notoriously "bolshie" (as we would have said) organizations like the Royal Army Education Corps, often proved to have a more critical and original approach, particularly in all forms of the social sciences, including history. A little astonished by our good fortune, we took our studies seriously; I remember being surprised and even outraged when the Junior Common Room acquired a television set. The attention now given by many universities to "leisure activities" would have seemed to us misplaced; if not downright inappropriate. We all tended to look a little tattered, wearing the remains of bits of our uniforms; I for instance had a jeep-coat that served well for many years in the bitter Cambridge winters, and later in Paris.

Our accommodation in college left much to be desired, by modern standards. There was a contemporary story of two American matrons, visiting one of the ancient colleges, with one remarking in surprise to the other, "say, these ruins are inhabited." The Old Court in Corpus was not as bad as that, but, having remained the same for about six hundred years, it did lack efficient heating and any plumbing; indeed, the bathroom block lay across the grassy court from my room (2). We took all our meals in college, for we had been accustomed to eating together in some form of mess, and very few of us knew how to cook, in sharp contrast to the coming generation of young men.

We got about the place on bicycles, for undergraduates were not allowed to have cars, and few of us could anyway afford such a luxury. Many afternoons we would ride our bikes to one of the magnificent playing-fields on the outskirts of town, for games of hockey, cricket and rugby against teams from other colleges. CCC had a particularly large and well-appointed field, though as a small college our teams were often beaten by those of larger colleges. In the summer, though, the teas prepared by our groundsman for cricket matches were unbeatable. As I explained in the previous chapter, I also spent a good deal of time either at the headquarters of the University Air Squadron, out on the Trumpington Road, or else at Marshall's airfield; flying pay was an essential part of my budget.

(2) In the Old Court, no doubt on the way to the bathroom across the court.

Lectures were offered by the History Faculty of the University, but tutorials – the most essential part of the system – were provided by the College. CCC had at the time four historians, Patrick Bury, Christopher Cheney, John Roach and Richard Vaughan; we rarely used their Christian names. We saw most of John and Richard, the more junior Fellows, going to tutorials with one of them once a week. The aim of these tutorials, very well expressed lately by the Chancellor, Lord Sainsbury, was to teach us to "assimilate a mass of information, pull out of it the key issues and then produce coherent and persuasive arguments on the basis of the evidence." The latter part of this exercise was as important as the former, for as Tony Judt puts it, in *The Memory Chalet* (New York, 2010), "for many centuries in the Western tradition, how well you expressed a position corresponded closely to the credibility of your argument;" we surely were heirs to this perhaps faulty tradition.

We were also heirs to a long tradition of hospitality between teachers and pupils. Our rooms were on staircases, a dozen or so of us, and there too would be found the rooms of one of the College Fellows. He was in effect what has come to be called a "counsellor", often asking his charges round to sherry, and generally keeping an eye on them. During my first year, the Fellow on my staircase was Tom Faber, a low-temperature physicist who also played a part in the publications of his family firm, the well-known Faber and Faber, where T.S. Eliot once worked. I see from my diaries that we also had a lively social life with the junior History Fellows, constantly drinking coffee or sherry with them, and attending concerts and plays together. Indeed, they became friends of many of us for the rest of our lives.

My fellow-historians were a varied group. Peter came from a family long established in the tea business, based in London. He eventually went into the family business, working for a while in Assam; he spent the second half of his life running an Anglican agency for low-cost housing in London. Christopher, a Suffolk man like myself, was a farmer's son who went into Shell Oil, where he rose high, working for some years on the then new Alaska pipeline. Gerald came from Norfolk, and always wanted to join the British civil service. Indeed, he passed out very high in the civil service examination and spent part of his life introducing computerization to various government agencies.

As we were almost all able to attend the University because of state scholarships, we seem to have had a curious sense of *noblesse oblige*. None of us thought of going into the City, believing on the whole that while it was not bad to be rich, wealth was best acquired either by birth or by life's accidents, and not by dubious financial operations. Perhaps we would have called that "money-grubbing," now an entirely outdated phrase. We had one companion from the United States, Denny Mayer, who came to Corpus after a first degree at Amherst. He belonged to a family of Chicago lawyers, and eventually joined the family firm. Denny brought a novel set of attitudes from across the Atlantic, including the unforgettable songs of Tom Lehrer ("Midst the sage-brush and the cactus/I'll watch the fellas practus/ Droppin bombs through the clear desert breeze/ O, I'll soon make my appearance/ Soon as I can get my clearance/For the Wild West is where I wanna be").

We were also close to the Senior Tutor, Michael McCrum, a classicist who had a very distinguished career, eventually becoming headmaster of Eton College and then Master of Corpus. Michael had a deceptively languid and patrician manner (his father being a captain in the Royal Navy) which invited practical jokes. On one occasion, finding that he had asked us to see him too early in the morning, we appeared in our dressing-gowns (3).

(3) Paying an early-morning visit to the Senior Tutor (from the left, Peter, myself, John, Christopher and Andrew).

I chiefly saw Patrick Bury at this time because I had become undergraduate assistant in the Parker Library, of which he was Librarian. This library contained (and contains) many priceless manuscripts, often collected from monastic libraries seized in the 1530s by Henry VIII. Our operation now seems a little informal. I remember that once some visiting scholar asked to see our edition of René Descartes' *Discours de la Méthode* (an immensely rare and valuable publication, printed at Paris in 1637). Patrick telephoned me when I was in the library, and asked me to get the Descartes out, explaining that it could be found on a lower shelf, where it would be partly obscured by some other vellum-bound volume, that would not quite fit on the shelf. Following these directions, I found the Descartes quite easily; oddly, we do not seem to have inflicted serious damage, or to have lost anything of value. Indeed, there was a standing legally-binding penalty if we lost anything; then the whole collection would have passed to another college, just down King's Parade.

The academic system required a good deal of personal discipline from undergraduates. As we only took examinations at the end of the year, it was possible to coast along for many months, until the dread month of May, if you were willing to disregard warning shots from the tutors, including eventually a sharp letter from McCrum (no question of the lugubrious practice of "continuous assessment" by frequent tests). Of course, if you failed your exams you were "sent down" (dismissed); that was that. Examination-papers were set by anonymous members of the faculty, and we took them over the course of a week or so, with three-hourly sessions each morning and afternoon. They were then marked equally anonymously, with no nods to "instructor's autonomy." Our tutors thus became in a sense our allies against the examiners and did not have constantly to sit in judgment on our efforts. If we put in a feeble essay, their job was to encourage improvements, but not primarily to assess.

The History Faculty had a set of lecturers, but we did not think it necessary to attend all these offerings, simply tasting them at will. I see from one diary-entry that I attended a "Lecture by Bennett: Oh, the boredom!" Some of the lecturers were well-known characters, like John Saltmarsh of Trinity College, who in lecturing on early English economic history each year brought out his model of a fulling-mill, to sustained applause. Professor Walter Ullman, a refugee from Vienna, entranced us with his accent, observing on one occasion, à propos of medieval times (which he thought under-appreciated) that "if zey was fools, we iz bluddy fools." I also attended the earliest lectures on European early modern history of John Elliott of Trinity College. His exposition was a model; clear, logical and taking into account the most recent research. He eventually became director of the Institute for Advanced Studies at Princeton, in the United States, and later on Regius Professor at Oxford. We have long remained friends, partly through the Society for the History of Discoveries.

Few of my friends had any interest in the Cambridge Union. I only remember going there once, and that was at the time of the Suez affair. For 30 October 1956, my diary notes that "Britain/France are playing the fool in Egypt." After their invasion many Corpuscles expressed their strong opposition to it, and I seem to remember that we accompanied our token Egyptian student - whom I am afraid that we called "Wog," to his apparent amusement - to the Union, so that he could in tranquillity make a fierce speech against the renewed incursion into his country. I remembered then, too, that a few months previously (while playing cricket) I had noticed a convoy of military vehicles painted desert tan in Bury Saint Edmunds, an army base just to the east; the preparations for this so-called emergency had been made quite far in advance.

Corpus is just round the corner from Fisher House, the Catholic chaplaincy. This was led by Canon Gilbey, of the gin family. He had a wonderful Iberian accent, and a devoted following among the students. I seem to remember having a splendid lunch with him at the Bath Hotel, which was next door to the Corpus home pub, the "Eagle." Here one could drink Greene, King Ale from Bury Saint Edmunds, and admire the graffiti on the ceiling, mostly left by members of the United States Army Air Force, whose heavy bombers had been based during the Second World War at the nearby airfields of Mildenhall and Lakenheath. These remained US bases for many years after the war, and their presence at the time of the Cuba missile crisis in 1961 led even the least nervous of us to glance from time to time to the east, wondering if a mushroom cloud might appear there. USAF Lakenheath was also the source of a great Corpus triumph.

Each year the colleges competed to see who could collect most money for Poppy Day, November 11th, Armistice Day from 1918. Traditionally, we would unimaginatively harass car-drivers until they put something in our collection-tins. But my friend Christopher, budding entrepreneur, had a better idea; why not, he said, organize a game of American football between the two US bases, and hold it on the University rugby ground at Grange Road, charging a small entry fee to this spectacle? We thought that he was out of his mind, but the Americans were amenable, and the scheme worked astonishingly well. Corpus handily won the competition that year and the next.

We were in general quite out of touch with the problems of the country at large. One echo which did reach us came from engineering friends who sometimes spent the summer on internships for firms producing cars. They uniformly returned with tales of appalling labour relations, which led to good designs being sloppily manufactured and then even worse supported by after-sales service. Most of us, though, did not do anything so practical with our summers.

(4) Lunch with Peter Warren and Christopher Wright, outside Sens, France.

For my part, after putting in a good many hours flying with the Air Squadron at summer camp, where we generally stayed in the sumptuous buildings constructed during the rearmament drive of the late 1930s, I went with car-owning friends to tour parts of France, Spain and Italy (4). Spain was still in the grip of General Franco, and in parts like Murcia, where republican spirit ran high, there was a heavy military presence, including aircraft (Messerschmitt 109s) which flew very low and threateningly overhead. At Tarragona, where it was wet, I foolishly tried to dry my little tent by lighting a spirit-stove inside it. The stove exploded, blowing my eyebrows off, but luckily without blinding me. As I sat outside, trying to gather my senses, a German camper came out of a nearby tent. Looking at me without much sympathy, "People in tents fires should not light," he remarked; how right he was. In our planning, most of us hardly thought of venturing outside Europe, so that our travels would seem absurdly parochial to modern students.

Towards the end of our third year, we began to think about what to do next. As historians, we did not have any specific professional qualification, and toyed with a number of possibilities. Some of us, especially language students, were silently recruited by gentlemen from London, and disappeared into organizations like MI 5 and MI 6. A few of us, like Peter, went into family firms. Many of us went to London and took the extensive written examination for the British civil or foreign service. From the "table of results" for 1958, I see that most of us fell into the category of "not invited for further tests." I did appear among the 200 or so "invited to attend the Civil Service Selection Board," but after a fairly disastrous interview (I did not have strong or coherent views about the situation in South Africa), I received a splendidly bureaucratic letter telling me that among surviving candidates I was one of those "certain to be unsuccessful" (5).

CIVIL SERVICE COMMISSION
6 Burlington Gardens, London w.1
Telephone: REGent 6010 Ext.

Ex/T/2   24th March, 1958.

Dear Sir,

As the final interviews in the open competitions for the Administrative Class and the Senior Branch of the Foreign Service by Method II go on for about two months, the Commissioners wish to give every candidate some indication of his position as soon as possible after his interview.

2.   The Commissioners cannot at this stage say whether a candidate will be successful, because the number of vacancies is limited and selection is competitive, and they are reluctant to give information which might prove misleading. They have therefore decided to divide candidates into three categories:-

(A) those who, on the assumption that the number of vacancies and the standard of competition prove to be about the same as in recent years, will be successful;

(B) those who, on the same assumption as at (A), are at or near the border-line;

(C) those who are certain to be unsuccessful.

3.   You are in category ..C... for the Administrative Class, and category ..C... for the Foreign Service.

/4.

(5) Letter from the Civil Service Commission, letting me know
that I was "certain to be unsuccessful" in their competition.

However, the written test did have a certain use. I was no great shakes on the papers concerning mathematics or general intelligence, but I did score very highly in the papers based on language analysis, significance and composition, and this assessment offered some guidance for the future. Some of my friends who had not fared well were determined not to be downhearted, and organized celebrations, secretly relieved, perhaps, at not having to become organization men. In general, it was thought bad form to take either success or failure too seriously. I cannot see us, like the graduating students at Harvard University, throwing our academic headwear high into the air, at the prospect of giddy riches in the City/ Wall Street. Instead, I see that one of my friends invited me to celebrate "A Failure" that February (6). Indeed, almost any occasion could be the excuse for a party. David Ramsbotham, who later became a most distinguished soldier and then civil servant, held a party at which his guests did not at first recognize each other. It was only after the introductions began that the light dawned: "Mr. Longbotham, may I introduce you to Dr. Sidebottom," and so forth.

David Buisseret, esq.

Hugh Davidson

invites you to join him in celebrating

A Failure

on Sunday, Feb. 2, at 12.15 p.m.

R.S.V.P. Corpus Christi

Champagne

Dress : Informal

NB. Top hats will be worn

(6) Invitation from Hugh Davidson, to celebrate a failure.

After my encounter with the Civil Service Selection Board, it was back to the University's Appointments Board. There was a story that one candidate, for whom an interview had been arranged with a US-based firm, was confronted by a Yankee tycoon who opened the proceedings by remarking, "Wal, boy, sell yourself." We were not good at that, no doubt valuing understatement excessively, and generally believing that less can well be more. As the term approached its end, I thought increasingly that perhaps I would try and join the regular Royal Air Force, which at the time was introducing all kinds of interesting new aircraft, including the range of V-bombers: the Valiant, Victor and Vulcan.

This was the situation when on 16 June 1958 the marks for the Tripos (Examination) Finals were posted. Lacking the courage to scan the boards at the Senate House myself, I see that I asked my good friend James Kerr (later a prominent figure in the British Council) to look for me. As the diary for that day records, "Sent James Kerr to look at the board – O Miracle! I had a First, so Dr. Roach and Richard [Vaughan] came in to celebrate and we had a merry time."

In Corpus, there had been no question of staying on to work for a higher degree unless one had a First, preferably in both years. But even so my mentors encouraged me to think in terms of a doctorate in history. Patrick Bury even had an idea for a subject. As we sipped his sherry one evening, he mentioned that in Paris the National Archives had recently acquired a large deposit of hitherto unexamined papers concerning Sully, chief minister of Henri IV of France (1589-1610). "Well, Patrick," I said, "that sounds like a good idea." Now was the time to find out who this "Sully" was.

7

First steps in research: Cambridge and Paris, 1958-1961

Preparations for a doctorate in history in my day at Cambridge tended to be a rather hit-and-miss affair. As Corpus had no specialist in early modern European history, I was assigned to Outram Evennett in Trinity College, and to Charles Wilson of Jesus College. Evennett, alas, was mortally ill, and so could play little part, while Wilson, a specialist in the economic history of early modern Europe, often seemed preoccupied by events on the Newmarket race-track, some twenty miles to the east, as I sat idly in his lovely rooms in Jesus College. As a result, I largely prepared myself for research in France by intensive reading in the University Library.

The library had long ago received the collection of Lord Acton, a distinguished Cambridge professor of history of the late nineteenth century, and so it contained a good many otherwise unobtainable works on French history. It also had an almost unique and wonderful tool: the printed inventories of virtually all the French provincial archives, from great cities like Amiens and Dijon, but also from quite obscure little towns. These inventories were available in long rows on open shelves in the reading room, and so allowed one to plan research-campaigns in the French provinces. To my knowledge, the only other set of this massive publication in England was at the British Library. But there it lay barely catalogued and quite unused in a back room, as I one day saw.

The University Library had an ingenious cataloguing system. As it received books, it listed these on a printed monthly publication. Librarians then cut out the author-reference for each of these books and pasted it into a long series of huge alphabetically-ordered volumes ranged each side of the "catalogue room." This meant that you could only approach books through this alphabetical list of authors, and also that the assistants had to judge how much space to leave for future publications by each author. Of course, this archaic system has long been replaced by a more easily searchable electronic arrangement.

In general, my training compared very unfavorably with that of my friends from the United States, whom I met in Paris. They had generally had to sit special examinations on the general history of the area they meant to study, to learn at least one supplementary language, and often to take a course in paleography (the study of ancient writing) and in the editing of texts. I did have some knowledge of French and German, and eventually picked up some Spanish and Italian. But this was quite informal, as were my studies in paleography, which took the form of working over books with adjacent texts in ancient writing and modern transcriptions. These were lent to me by French friends who had survived the stringent French training in this field at the École des Chartes, the school for reading and interpreting early texts.

Corpus research students in those days lived in a series of former family houses on the western edge of town, each with a grandmotherly warden who cooked for us. In fact, Michael McCrum and kindred spirits were at that time in the process of setting up the adjacent Leckhampton House, which became the graduate housing (1). This fine nineteenth-century manor-house lay in a superb garden, and eventually offered – and offers – an unrivalled place for graduate students (often from outside the UK) to live and work in a congenial and sometimes usefully critical community.

(1) Leckhampton House, which was about to become
the hostel for Corpus research students.

From the autumn of 1958 to the early summer of 1959, I spent most days in the University Library. My walk there led past Selwyn College, home of many Anglican ordinands, and I still remember the delightful music (mostly nineteenth-century hymns) which would float from their chapel. When the cricket season came, I often went to Bury St Edmunds, thirty miles to the east, to play for the "Gentlemen of Suffolk", an unfashionably-named team which brought together all kinds of people: local farmers, soldiers from the nearby garrison, colonial officials on leave and so forth. If the game lasted two days over the weekend, we often spent the Saturday night dancing in some local person's house. They were very kind to an impoverished student like me; I remember that once my host lent me his Jaguar to attend early Mass in Bury St Edmunds. I also recall that one of our oldest members, Colonel Kryer, still a useful fast bowler, had served as a young man on India's northwestern frontier, and could on occasion be persuaded to talk about encounters with the Waziris, whose military skills he greatly respected.

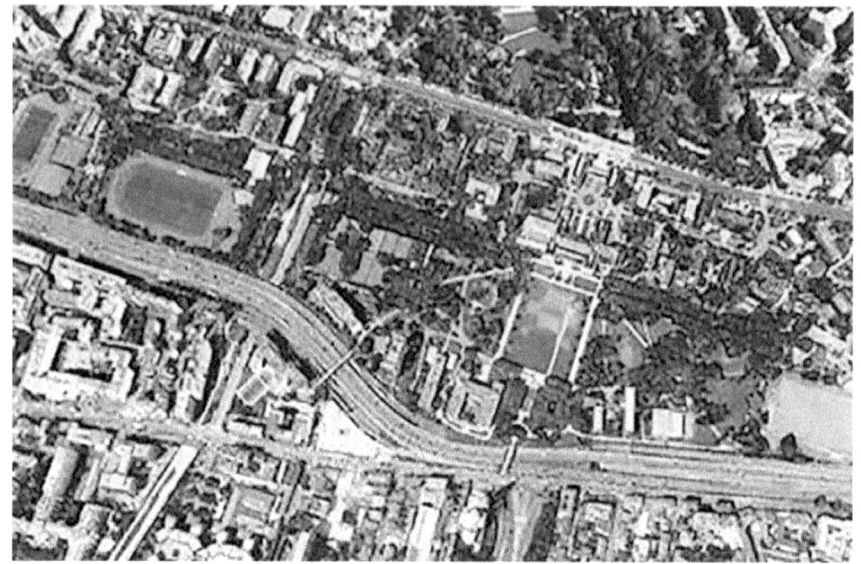

(2) Aerial view of the *Cité Universitaire*, sandwiched between the old east-west boulevard to the north, and the new expressway to the south. The central building, with its large if rather brown lawn, is surrounded by the *pavillons* of the various countries.

By the fall of 1959, I was ready to go to Paris. The best place to stay seemed to be the University City (*Cité Universitaire*), a great complex of student housing at the southern edge of Paris. The Cité had been founded, in the 1920s, on a section of the former fortifications of Paris, which were being dismantled after the war to end all wars (2). Each country in the world – though not at first including Germany – was invited to build a *pavillon*, and then this building would house a mixture of students: half of them from France, and the rest mostly from the country in question. Some very distinguished architects were commissioned to build these student hostels: the *Maison de la Suisse* (The Swiss house) for example, was the work of Le Corbusier. My *pavillon* was the *Franco-Britannique*, known as "the Franco-B."

(3) The *Cité's* main building, conceived in the style of a French *château*.

The *Cité* had – and has – a fine central building (3), with a swimming-pool and dining-hall and library, as well as offices. The dining-hall was often the scene of joyful rowdiness; for instance, anybody entering it wearing a hat would be greeted by loud shouts of *"chapeau"* until the hat was doffed. The *Cité* had a wonderful cultural life, for many students were accomplished musicians, who had come to study at the Paris *Conservatoire*; almost every night one or other of the fifty or so *pavillons* would offer concerts by them. The *Cité* also had a great deal of jocular "public art." One poster that I particularly liked was the work of the women's basketball association. A previous year's player having married the Shah of Persia, the new year's poster read: *"Basketteurs, joignez-nous: tous les espoirs vous sont permis"* ("Basketball players, join us; anything is possible"). Alas, this marriage, like the regime, did not end well.

The *Cité* was on the Paris *Métro*, or underground railway, and its station lay on the edge of the lovely Parc Montsouris, which had been converted from a quarry in the city-planning days of baron Haussmann, in the mid-nineteenth century. You could catch a train here and eventually emerge in central Paris. My path took me for many months north to the stop called "Les Halles." Here, in those days, you emerged into a wonderfully malodorous series of huge hangars, in which vegetables had been on sale since the dawn. Watching over the market was the church of Saint-Eustache, whose choir sometimes gave superb recitals of the great early modern religious composers like Josquin des Prez and Luis Vittoria. A few streets away was the Bibliothèque Nationale, or National Library (now the "Bibliothèque nationale de France"). Much of it built in the nineteenth century, it had a superb eighteenth-century reading-room where you could call up the many manuscripts that contained the history of France in the days of Sully. If the writing was very tricky, you could in those days ask one of the presiding archivists for help; it was rarely possible to stump them. If you tired of the *Métro*, you could take a bus. In those days the buses had open rear platforms, and it was possible to catch them in flight, as it were, by sprinting up behind them and jumping onto the platform, often to a variety of remarks from the other passengers.

Sully's memoirs, first published in the middle of the seventeenth century, formed two massive, printed volumes, of which the most accessible subsequent edition had been published in the early nineteenth century. Having bought a copy of this highly concentrated but still 1,200-page document in two volumes, I began making an index of its contents, since this would clearly be the best way to approach so forbidding a text. One evening, when I was hard at work on this task in the library of the *Cité*, I noticed a very pretty girl also hard at work nearby. No Lothario, I did not usually approach young women. But for some reason I felt impelled to talk to this one, interrupting her work. I wrote in my diary, "she is an American, called Patricia Connolly." I saw her again at Mass the next Sunday, and we began to form part of a group of students who attended the University Chaplaincy, housed in a smaller stylistic version of the Montmartre cathedral. It lay across the expressway which hemmed the *Cité* into the south, and it maintained a lively social life. Every Sunday one of the *pavillons* would provide a lunch for the rest; we ate some remarkable food like that. We also had a lively choir, drawing on a wide variety of talents, and sometimes went to sing in the remarkably decrepit old people's home in nearby Kremlin-Bicêtre (its name coming from a period of French enchantment with the Soviet Union). We went as a group to the annual pilgrimage at Chartres, whose magnificent cathedral lay seventy miles or so to the southwest, across innumerable wheatfields (4).

(4) Flyer for the Chartres pilgrimage, 1960.

After I had worked for a month or two in Paris, one of my French friends invited me to the "Bal de l'École des Chartes," or annual dance of the great French archival school. We danced for the night at the Archives' eighteenth-century palace in the Marais quarter, and then had the traditional onion soup in the Halles, where the day's vegetables were just arriving. In the course of conversation, I told my companion, Madeleine, that I was working on Sully. "But," she replied, "do you not know that Bernard Barbiche has just finished his thesis at the École on this subject?" Bernard was the first in his class, and his thesis was clearly not to be despised; alarmed, I went to see him. We became fast friends and have worked jointly on various projects in French history ever since then.

In fact, my studies were quite unfashionable. Enterprising students from England and the United States generally went to study, if they could, with fashionable and often left-wing professors like Fernand Braudel, author of a widely-acclaimed study of the Mediterranean in early modern history. I went instead to Roland Mousnier, an excellent scholar but by no means a fashionable one; indeed, he was a Catholic, and knew all about the sale of offices in the time of Henri IV (1589-1610). Reading the memoirs of Patrick Collinson, once Regius Professor of History at Cambridge, I find a succinct but accurate expression of my (our) approach to history: "To be sure, antiquarianism is never enough. What is more required? In my case, not what is called 'theory' and sometimes 'grand theory.' I do not think that the study of the past can produce 'theory.'" We were far from the vaulting ambitions of the Braudelians.

However, that did not prevent me from being entirely seduced by the wide-ranging ideas of Marc Bloch, in some sense the forerunner of Braudel. Bloch, active in the Resistance, had been caught and killed by the Germans in 1941, but left several books in which he set out his ideas. Primary among these was the insistence that too much written "history" consisted of political events, and that these made no sense unless they were related to simultaneous economic, social and cultural developments. I tried to apply Bloch's principles, though probably with little success.

Having laid a good foundation in the Bibliothèque Nationale, I ventured into the other libraries of Paris: the Archives Nationales, the Affaires Étrangères and so forth. One of the most fruitful such ventures was into the attics of the Invalides (a superb hospital for veterans, founded in the seventeenth century), where a huge collection of very dusty models of French towns remained from the time of Louis XIV, often including the work of the engineers of Henri IV, completed in the early seventeenth century. This was long before these models had been spruced up and presented as the "Musée des Plans-Reliefs," a wonderful museum which now gives the visitor the impression of flying over French towns as they were three hundred years ago. This first campaign in Paris proved to be the first of many. I came to understand the sentence of Ernest Hemingway in *A Moveable Feast*: "If you are lucky enough to have lived in Paris as a young man, then wherever you go for the rest of your life it stays with you, for Paris is a moveable feast."

After the autumn of 1959 I began visiting the rest of France, mainly the great cities that had been the provincial capitals in Sully's day: Amiens for Picardy, Caen for Normandy, Dijon for Burgundy, Toulouse for Languedoc and so forth. In these capitals could be found the letters sent by Sully in his (remarkably successful) efforts to reform the finances of France. In these visits I was much helped by the contacts provided by the Jesuit François de Dainville and by General Nicolas, formerly of the engineering arm of the French army. I went to see Father de Dainville at the house of the Jesuit periodical, *Les Études*, and well remember his excitement as he unrolled a spool of microfilm that I had brought from London. As the film curled onto the floor, coursing down his black soutane to his great black boots, he constantly exclaimed things like "tiens, c'est magnifique"; these drawings by French engineers of the time of Henri IV, preserved at the British Library, were indeed very original and then quite unknown. General Nicolas offered less austere hospitality in one or two of the French army messes in Paris. He had many useful contacts, and was curiously favorable towards the Anglo-saxons, and not at all pleased by General de Gaulle's hostility to them.

In those days, the aim of a historian trained like me was to identify a coherent theme, and then to read everything relevant to it. Many more recent themes would not have seemed to us coherent; we would not have known what to do with titles like (it is, I hope, invented, but typical) "*Politics, War and Love in Mazarin's France.*" This all-enveloping ambition of ours could lead to some demanding situations; at Christmas 1959, for instance, M. Mousnier was not keen that I return to England for that holiday, since, as he put it, I "might miss reading something." At all events, the material slowly took shape. Bernard's thesis for the École des Chartes had primarily concerned financial matters, so I extended my work to include Sully's activity on the communications (roads and canals), artillery, fortifications and navy of the reign of Henri IV (1589-1610). At this time Bernard and I also began work on an edition of the memoirs of Sully, published by the *Société de l'Histoire de France*. Our first volume received a prize from the *Institut de France*, and we have just finished the fourth volume, which carries the story up to 1604.

English students in Paris often made ends meet by undertaking work like translation and coaching. I translated several manuals for Vélosolex, a manufacturer of small motor-cycles. Most of their vehicles went to India, and I have sometimes wondered what the mechanics of Delhi made of my work, confused as the text already was. My main student was Giles, the son of former Group Captain Peter Townsend, who had had an unhappy affair with princess Margaret. I occasionally visited the Townsends in their flat on the Quai Blériot; he must even then have been writing his excellent history about the Battle of Britain, *Duel of Eagles*, published in 1969. Alas, I do not know how successful my coaching efforts with Giles may have been. Perhaps in this respect I am like the British Museum attendant, who could remember that in his day there had been an assiduous reader called Karl Marx, but said that he did not know what had become of this quiet and hardworking patron.

As the year wore on, I began to see more and more of Pat. After graduating in French and history from Marquette University in Milwaukee, she had taught for a year at a high school in Chicago. But feeling that her oral French was inadequate for this task, she had no difficulty in saving enough money over the year to fund a year at the Sorbonne. Those were the days of what one Trinidadian calypsonian later called "the mighty dollar bill;" Pat did not need to think in those days about what plays or meals cost, and we did see wonderful theatre by playwrights like Ionesco, as well as sometimes eating like royalty. These ventures were not helpful for my work, and I see several diary entries reading something like "met Pat at supper and did little work after that." Sometimes, indeed, we would spend several hours walking the three or four miles back from the banks of the Seine to the *Cité*; "O temps, suspends ton vol…" The year was coming to a close, and we needed to think about the future. In the end, neither of us could imagine a future without the other, and so we agreed that she would return to the United States but then come to Cambridge as soon as possible. From Chicago, she sent me a photograph which ought to have warned me about the weather in the Midwest (5)

(5) Pat in Chicago, about Christmas of 1960.

She eventually came over in February 1961, when I see from the diary that at Heathrow we had "trouble with the immigration officer." In fact, I am amazed that he let her in, on my slightly hesitant assurance that we intended to get married; he must have been more kindly than others I have known.

(6) Pat meets my parents in Woodbridge, early in 1961.

We soon went to Woodbridge, so that Pat could meet my parents and brother (6 and 7), and then settled back into Cambridge, where Pat shared a house with some young women from Bahrain. She quite easily found illegal work with a kindly estate agent, where she was paid out of petty cash (her wages being, indeed, petty). We then ate most evenings together at Fanshawe House, my hostel just by the emergent Leckhampton, run by Mrs. Meggison. Meanwhile the thesis made good progress, and in April I was able to submit the nine chapters not only to the University Board, but also to the Fellowship Committee in Corpus. In those days, I took seriously the adage of Nicolas Boileau (1636-1711) that "qui ne sait se borner ne sut jamais écrire" (somebody who did not know how to restrain himself never knew how to write). This made for a very tight and succinct thesis, but I ought to have widened its scope for the subsequent book, published in 1968 (*Sully*). As one of my West Indian colleagues later remarked, in a cricketing metaphor, "David, why do you never open your shoulders?" (i.e. venture wider-ranging, more original and probably less verifiable arguments).

(7) My brother Christopher ("Kit"). Born in 1945, he attended RMA Sandhurst, and is here seen during his training as a helicopter pilot with the Royal Artillery.

About this time, too, I went to the University of Bristol to be interviewed for a post in the Department of History there. This was a fairly harrowing process. After sending in an application, if you were selected for interview you went to Bristol on the appropriate day, together with half a dozen other candidates. At the Department, we all sat on a long bench outside the interview room, exchanging nervous banter before we were called before the committee. Eventually one of us was chosen, and the rest of us were left to lick our wounds, or maybe solace ourselves with good West Country cider. In fact, I did not have to fret for long, as in May 1961 I was elected to a Research Fellowship at Corpus, together with Michael Tanner, with whom I had simultaneously arrived on the platform of Cambridge station in September 1955. The Fellowship began in September; meanwhile I had to get married.

Pat and I flew to the United States on July 4th, using a very interesting aircraft called a "Bristol Britannia," one of a generation of machines that used "turboprops," jet engines driving propellers. In those days even economy passengers had quite a lot of room, and transatlantic crossings were not unpleasant. Arriving in Chicago, we moved into the house in Skokie where John and Helen Connolly lived with their other three daughters. They were almost an archetypal Chicago family, Irish on John's side and Polish on Helen's. John was very Irish in character, with a wonderful store of tall tales, and some sizzling one-liners, like "get wise to yourself." Helen was a very tall, elegant woman, who could still dance a mean Charleston; she was also John's accountant. The fact that neither had gone to a university testified, perhaps, to the waste of talent in those days.

John ran a business providing fire-equipment services to local institutions, and I became one of his assistants for the summer. I soon realized that this business, like many others, was not quite what it seemed. John was a very clubbable Irishman, friends with many of the local (often Irish) fire-captains. They played a certain role in the business; often they could, for instance, be persuaded to enact a by-law that all curtains in local businesses had to be fire-proofed. This, of course, meant that many lucrative sets of curtains would come into our workshop to be soaked in some noxious chemical.

My companion in this work was Otto Zorn, a young immigrant from Augsburg, Germany. Innocent of any regulations, we handled many risky chemicals in the course of refilling the standard fire-extinguisher, which had then to be exchanged for outdated ones. Even more dangerous was the process of filling pressurized extinguishers. For this you dropped "dry ice" into a tall and very robust cylinder, and when the ice "melted" (under high pressure), you could tap the resultant gas at a series of spigots. You had to be careful about this, though, because the cylinders that we thus filled could escape your grasp in the process, and then Otto and I would have to take hasty cover under a stout bench, while the errant cylinder whizzed round the workshop. Our operation definitely did not conform to more recent ideas about safety.

Observing Otto and his friends, I was very impressed by the way in which at that time in the United States a young person with only a high school diploma could thrive, earning enough not only to support a family, but also to send a child or two to the (excellent) local state university, and even one day buy a little vacation-cabin up north in Wisconsin. All this would change in the Reagan years, which set in during the 1980s; thirty years later, most laboring families needed two wage-earners even to scrape by.

Coming from an England which was still fairly depressed, I was amazed by the profusion of goods, not only in the great department stores like Marshall Field's, but also in the newly-emerging "shopping centers" like Old Orchard. There was also a profusion of free public entertainment, including not only the concerts given at Grant Park, but also the lunchtime "Dame Myra Hess" concerts offered at the Chicago Public Library, in a huge room whose splendid translucent roof had been the work of the stained-glass master Louis Tiffany.

Pat was a dutiful daughter, and I an obedient son-in-law. So we played little part in the planning of our wedding, which took place in the church of Saint Margaret Mary, where Pat had been to elementary school, on 9 September 1961 (8). My best man was Corpuscle Denny Mayer, a lawyer in Chicago, and some of our English friends (mostly from Corpus) sent us a witty telegram (9). We then left for our honeymoon in New York. Times Square, very dilapidated in those days, was a poor choice, but we needed to be there in order to catch the *Queen Mary*. In fact, we were so disorganized and feckless that we narrowly caught the great ship, arriving, to the astonishment of one seaman, just as the last gang-plank was being hauled aboard (10).

(8) Our marriage in Chicago, September 1961.

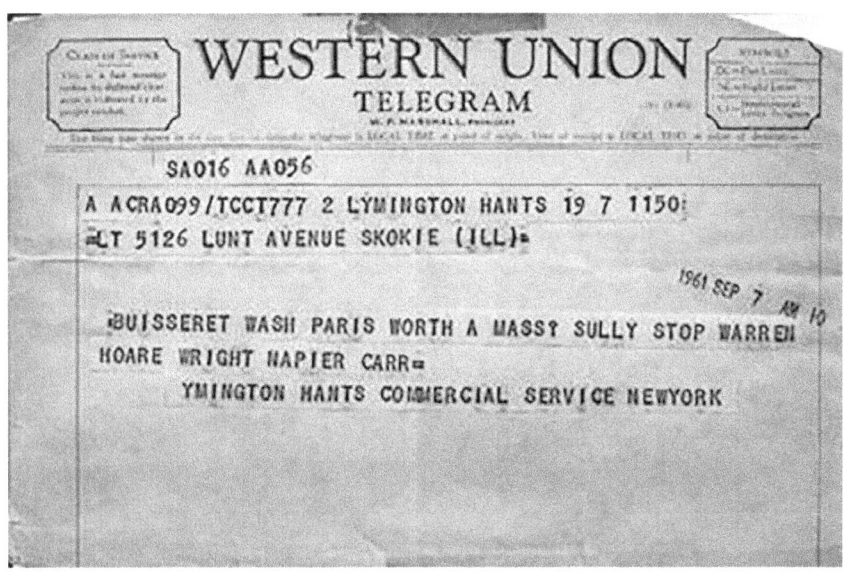

(9) A wedding telegram from Peter, Christopher, Tim Hoare, Dennis
Napier and Anthony Carr. When he converted to Catholicism
in 1594, Henri of Navarre is said to have remarked "Paris is well
worth a Mass." So my friends ask if this was so in my case...

I see that our cabin was "D42, down in the bowels;" a cheap passage
on the *Queen Mary* was not to be recommended. We could only reach
the outer air on a small platform between the funnels, and the only air
reaching our cabin was distinctly second-hand. At all events, we made a
splendidly stormy crossing. Unimpressed by the application of the English
class system to sea-travel, we disembarked at Southampton and took the
train to Cambridge, where I could take up my fellowship at Corpus.

(10) The *Queen Mary* leaving New York, perhaps about 1965.

8

Research Fellow at Corpus Christi College, Cambridge, 1961-1964

It was an extraordinary opportunity, to be invited for three years to join the fifteen or so active Fellows of Corpus. They comprised a great range of talents. Our master, Sir George Paget Thomson (son of J.J. Thomson, leading atomic physicist around 1900), Nobel Prize winner in physics like his father, had led the British team which concluded in 1940 that an atomic weapon was possible, and had then been the leading liaison person with the Americans. At Corpus in the 1960s, Sir George was much preoccupied with the (still unsolved) problem of how to generate power through nuclear fusion. He had a huge fund of expertise, not only about aircraft, being an early experimental pilot and enthusiastic supporter of the Air Squadron, but also about ships, including the galleys of early seventeenth-century France that I studied. He was also full of good stories, like the one about when Corpus entertained one of the Dulles brothers, hearing from this Waspish Yankee that the "bog-Irish" Jack Kennedy, then early in his political career, would never amount to much. Sir George ran a tight College meeting, observing to Fellows who talked too much that he "seemed to have heard that before."

Entry to the Fellowship was a thoroughly medieval experience. In the chapel, and in the presence of the other Fellows, you knelt before the seated Master, put your clasped hands between his, and then recited in Latin the oath which bound you to offer the Master counsel and help ("consilium et auxilium"). This ceremony had surely not changed at that time for nearly six hundred years, though no doubt it has now faded out; indeed, the concept of a "Master" is now often unpalatable.

Some of the Fellows had been prisoners-of-war, when they had learned languages like Dutch, Italian and Japanese. Others again had worked on the decoding of the Enigma messages at Bletchley, though of course they never mentioned that. Sometimes, indeed, echoes of Bletchley came from unexpected places, as when we eventually learned that an otherwise unremarkable Woodbridge estate agent ("realtor") had been one of the intelligence sergeants who actually distributed the information gathered by the code-breakers, a crucial task.

The oldest fellow was Archie Clark-Kennedy, an enthusiastic if increasingly short-sighted cyclist into his eighties. He was a celebrated medical clinician and was writing a book about the English nurse Edith Cavell, shot by the Germans during the First World War as a spy. I tried in vain to find out anything about her from my Belgian aunts, nuns at Soignies; perhaps they knew that she really was a spy. Some Fellows were known for their eccentricity, including one who, finding face-to-face contact unbearable, would sometimes conduct his tutorials from under his desk. Relations with these Fellows could take a strange turn, as with my friend who met one of them in the New Court. The Fellow having asked where he (the Fellow) had been coming from, my friend replied that he had come from the northeast corner of the court. "Good," replied the Fellow, "I must have had lunch."

Every evening most of the Fellows would meet for dinner at high table in the dining-hall, with the undergraduates in the body of this elegant chamber. This was a great occasion for inviting one's colleagues (if they were men) to dine as guests, and indeed to meet the guests of other Fellows. Many of my French contacts thus came to dine in Corpus, including particularly Roger-Armand Weigert, in charge of the Prints and Drawings (which included much material from the time of Sully) at the Bibliothèque nationale de France. A member of the French Resistance, Weigert had been so tortured by the Gestapo that he was both deaf and dumb; one communicated with him by passing slips of paper, a novelty for the high table. After dinner the Fellows retired to the combination-room for port and madeira, where conversations could be continued. It was the task of the junior Fellow to keep track of the decanters and to polish off any which seemed moribund at the end of the evening. While I thus ate and drank in this unbridled fashion (getting rather stout) Pat sat at home with a baby or two; I consoled myself at the thought of this neglect by reflecting that we had spent the afternoon together, and that this state of affairs would not last forever. Occasionally she did attend a college dinner, once sitting next to Sir George, through some distant echo of the *droit du seigneur.* She has happy memories of what might have been a redoubtable encounter without the Master's kindness.

CORPUS CHRISTI COLLEGE, CAMBRIDGE
NAME DAY FEAST 1961

The Master, Fellows and Scholars
request the honour of the company of

FOR INFORMATION

at dinner on Thursday, 1 June, at 7.45 p.m. for 8 p.m.

Decorations
Doctors of the University will wear Scarlet

The favour of an early reply is requested
addressed to: The President, Corpus Christi
College, Cambridge

(1) My invitation to the Name Day feast, 1961.

The food on high table was good, and some of the young incoming Fellows felt that it was indeed too good, and so detracted from a better allocation of the College's assets. The periodic feasts were indeed lavish (1), but the general arrangements had emerged from a time when most of the Fellows were bachelors, and so had nowhere else sociably to eat; now the bachelors were beginning to be a minority. However, as I have explained, the possibility of inviting fellow scholars to dine could powerfully encourage all sorts of interdisciplinary contacts. Old members, too, were glad to renew their support of the College after some memorable feasts to which they had been invited; this fund-raising has become increasingly important.

The Fellows were divided roughly evenly between those who were married and bachelors. Some of the Fellows' wives were characters in their own right, about whom good stories were told. One of these concerned Mrs. Dickins, wife of Professor Bruce Dickins, with whom she shared a big house in Selwyn Gardens. After the war, some people in these large houses took in the families of undergraduates, ex-servicemen, who otherwise had nowhere to go. So, on one occasion a nervous Corpus undergraduate approached Mrs. Dickins, asking if she would consider taking him and his family in. Mrs. Dickins replied rather gruffly: "But do you have children?" The undergraduate confessed that he and his wife had two of them. "Oh good," replied Mrs. Dickins, "Do come in."

Sir George Paget Thomson was succeeded by Sir Frank Lee, who had been head of the British Civil Service. He had spent much time in the United States during the Second World War, and it fell to him, in Hall one evening in November 1963, to tell the Fellows and undergraduates assembled for dinner that President Kennedy had been wounded in Dallas. More recently tuned in, one undergraduate replied mournfully from the body of the hall, "he is dead, Master, he is dead." Sir Frank's wife, Lady Lee, was attentive to the perhaps neglected wives of the young Fellows; in particular, she would invite Pat to tea in her lovely Master's Lodge, so that Timothy could sleep in his pram in the garden. Pat also saw a lot of the wives of some of my new colleagues; Betty Bury was particularly welcoming to her, as was Margaret Vaughan, whose house on Lensfield Road was rapidly filling with children at the time, as ours would before long.

Our little house lay just across Botolph Lane from the high wall of the lodge (2).

(2) Pat in Botolph Lane with Tim in his pram. On the left is our car, under the wall of the Master's Lodge. Our little house was on the right; the Cavendish Laboratory can be seen at the end of the lane.

Here the College housed us in an early nineteenth-century workman's house, on four floors with a little room on each; the room at the top was a particular fire-trap, as there was no way of escape. It was only after some persuasion that the College agreed to install indoors plumbing; until then the lavatory was at the end of a little garden, in which we grew some rather hesitant flowers.

These negotiations must have taken place with the Steward of Estates, an organic chemist who had built a superb collection of nineteenth-century landscape aquatint views. At that time, posts like this Stewardship were always assigned to the Fellows, for they understood that if such posts went to professionals, then an ever-growing bureaucracy was likely to emerge, as indeed is the case in many modern universities, with their vice-presidents for security, for investments, for "institutional advancement" and so forth.

The old system was undoubtedly economical and fairly efficient, though it sometimes led to droll exchanges like the one I once heard. The Steward of Estates, elegant French scholar Patrice Charvet, was incensed at the suggestion that he consider raising the rent on some College property in Lincolnshire for, as he said, "My dear fellow, I already raised their rent twelve years ago; it is not yet time." Our lucky tenants came in once a year for a reckoning and a feast at which they were served Audit Ale...

Young Fellows were paid very little, for in a sense they were not supposed to be married (indeed, if they married as Fellows they were encouraged to pay a fine), and the College did provide them room and board. To make ends meet, we supervised undergraduates for tutorials, often from other Colleges. My most distinguished "student" was surely Christopher Andrew, who became a Fellow of Corpus and a leading expert on British secret services during the twentieth century. From Saint Catharine's came a student with a name famous in English history, even in the days of Shakespeare, and from Newnham the daughter of Victor Rothschild, a distinguished academic long and falsely suspected of being among the "Cambridge Five" spies, who included most notoriously Kim Philby.

From time to time, I would sit on college committees. One of the most interesting concerned admissions. It was often thought, in the Press and elsewhere, that Cambridge colleges were biased in favour of public schoolboys. In fact, nothing was further from the truth during my time on this committee; we were always looking for good candidates from state schools. But having often been rather poorly taught, it was hard for them to compete with public schoolboys who had often received excellent attention.

(3) Pat at our camp-site on the ramparts of Langres in northern France.

In 1962 Pat and I loaded up our little car, an Austin A35, to go to France so that I could work in the provincial archives and visit the sites of seventeenth-century building projects; palaces, canals, fortifications and so forth (3). We also took advantage of these visits for Pat to meet my Franciscan aunts (4), and also the cousins on the farm at Fontaine-Valmont (5).

(4) Pat with my Franciscan aunts at their convent in Soignies, Belgium.

(5) Yvonne and Marcel Bedoret with their daughter Kitty in
the farmyard of Le Sartalard, in southwestern Belgium.

The little car performed very well in country that was often rough. Once, when I took it to a French garage, the mechanic looked it over and then had a fine comment; "Eh, c'est pas beau mais c'est bien costaud" (it's not pretty, but it's mighty solid). In those days one did not hesitate to drive and park in Paris, and we often found cheap lodging on the left bank near the Place Furstenberg (6).

(6) The Place Furstenberg on the Left Bank in Paris, in the district where Pat and I used often to stay.

Our travels in France enabled me to finish a little monograph on the fortifications and other work of the French engineers in the reign of Henri IV. I wrote it up and submitted it to the University for the Alexander Prize. Curiously, Pat at that time worked in the Registry office responsible for administering these prizes. She told me – probably improperly – that no other entry had been received, and since it was the only entry, I hoped for the best. Alas, the assessors, professors Butterfield and Postan of Peterhouse, decided, without obtaining a competent report, that there would be no prize that year. Luckily, I was able quickly to translate this work and it was then at once published in the leading French journal on the theme, the *Bulletin de Géographie*. About this time my doctoral dissertation was approved by the Board of Research Studies. They did not require an oral examination, which has always seemed to me slightly improper.

Apart from spinning articles off from my thesis, I gave a series of public university lectures on the effect of war in forming the early modern state, a theme that has always interested me, and that surely would have become my central subject, had I stayed in England. Meanwhile the English publishers Eyre and Spottiswoode agreed to publish *Sully*, which came out in 1968. I slightly rewrote it, but without enough care and development to make it as accessible as possible to the general reader. This little book has remained the standard work in English on Sully, but it would have been much improved with careful expansion. Perhaps the theme was too seductive to an immature scholar. I felt that as the material was so original, being based entirely on newly-available material, that it spoke for itself: a mistake.

Among my guests at high table was a friend of Mr. Connolly from Chicago, Father James Larkin of De Paul University there. He was working on an edition of the proclamations of the Tudor monarchs, and from him I first heard of The Newberry Library in Chicago, which would eventually become the centre of my life and work. Meanwhile it was time to think about what we would do when my Fellowship ran out, in 1964. By then we had two children; Kate was born in 1964, joining Timothy who had arrived the previous year. Like many of my contemporaries, I had absolutely no idea about how to seek employment; indeed, we would have thought that "networking" was rather out of order. I did receive wonderful help from Eric Ceadel, Fellow in Japanese studies at the time; he showed me how to compose an impressive-looking *curriculum vitae*, to make the most of thin pickings.

By the spring of 1964 there were two possibilities: posts at the University of Wales in Aberystwyth, and at the University of the West Indies in Jamaica. To my continuing amazement, I received long handwritten letters from the heads of department in both of these universities; they must have been remarkably conscientious. Aberystwyth has a wonderful site on Cardigan Bay, and some prudent friends warned us that once you left Britain, it might not be easy to return. But I had long had West Indian friends, whom I admired in part for their laidback (as we would not have said) attitude to life, and the Jamaica campus was also exceptionally beautiful.

Moreover, the University, founded in 1958, was just entering upon a period of remarkably innovative research, not only in Caribbean history but also in West Indian literature and in such tropical scientific themes as high-altitude astronomy and natural-product chemistry. In addition, I was still under the influence of writers like John Buchan, who hoped that the Commonwealth "might be a potent and beneficent force in the world." Pat was not unwilling to participate (even with two tiny children) in an adventure which we thought might last for three or six years. So we decided on Jamaica.

After passing a fairly stiff physical examination (a sensible precaution which has gone out of fashion) I signed a contract with the Crown Agents, who then were acting for the University, and made plans to sail (with our little Austin, precariously lowered into the hull) on the *Camito*, a banana boat operated by Elder's and Fyffes. Wishing to introduce Tim and Kate to her parents, Pat arranged to fly through Chicago. Meanwhile we packed up the little house and left some of our furniture with friends in Cambridge. A Danish sofa which we rather liked thus spent fifty years in a tutor's room in Gonville and Caius College, until Jonathan Steinberg brought it back to us, when he eventually settled back in the United States in 2006. After a series of adventures, the sofa has ended up in Charlottesville, Virginia, with our daughter Claire. It now looks like an historic relic of postwar days, like us. My parents were of course not glad to see us leave, but we all thought that our stay across the Atlantic would be temporary.

Sometime about now Pat's parents, on a visit to Europe, came to see mine. This was a delightful occasion, enlivened by the odd misunderstanding. For instance, Pat having failed the (very difficult) English driving test, my father observed that she would have to study the Highway Code more closely, and perhaps take lessons. This was not Mr. Connolly's (or the Chicago) approach. Looking puzzled, he enquired more than once "yes, but who do you see?" Back home there would in those days surely have been an acquaintance (perhaps an Irishman) who could pull the necessary strings. Of course, you needed to know your man; otherwise you might be turned away with the traditional Chicago phrase; "nobody didn't send nobody."

In retrospect, I had been extraordinariy lucky to have held a Fellowship at Corpus in the final days of the ancient dispensation, when the Fellows were so few in number as to form a sort of family, with most of them attending High Table each night, and gladly taking up the various administrative tasks needed to run the College. The great expansion in numbers which took place in the 1960s was surely desirable on many different grounds, but it did destroy a social unit that had endured for many centuries. The new Fellows inevitably felt a primary loyalty rather to their departments and to the University than to the College, and this damaged its ancient cohesion. It was a remarkable experience, though, to have lived through things as they had long been. In spite of its popish name, Corpus had long been an Anglican institution, and I was perhaps the first practising Catholic to be a Fellow since the Reformation.

9

The University of the West Indies,
Jamaica Campus, 1964-1980

The *Camito*'s first stop in the West Indies was at Trinidad, and I knew at once what Alexander Humboldt meant, when upon arriving in the New World he remarked that he was "here in a divine country." Even a fine English day – and England never looked more attractive than when you were leaving it – could not compare with the vivid blues and greens of the sea and land into which one had been plunged; as Pat later put it, when we sadly left Jamaica, it was as if she had been snatched from a life lived in technicolor and found herself surrounded by monochrome. Entering the Caribbean Sea, the *Camito* made her way to Jamaica, where she docked at one of the Kingston finger-piers (1). In those days, before the construction of a new port, these lay at the end of Kingston's north-south streets, giving an extraordinary sense of scale to the urban landscape; it was as if one walked down a street and suddenly found oneself alongside a huge jet.

(1) Kingston piers about 1960; the *Camito* is one of
the two similar boats at the bottom right.

The University of the West Indies was – and is – a federal university with
campuses on other islands like Barbados and Trinidad, founded after the
Second World War, when the British belatedly understood the need for
tertiary education in their (soon to be former) West Indian colonies. The
campus at Mona, in the foothills of the Blue Mountains outside Kingston,
was the largest of the initial three campuses, and was sited on two former
sugar estates, Papine and Mona. During the war, these had held a camp
of people displaced from Malta and Gibraltar, and many of the buildings
from this time survived and were pressed into use. Many of them were very
sturdy, and for years examinations were held in one of the large wooden
huts, which seemed able to resist hurricanes. Some of the ruins from the
sugar plantations also survived, and the University's general plan worked
round these former structures. This plan consisted essentially of two ringroads, with the hospital occupying the middle of the northerly one, and
the Faculty of Arts taking up the other one. Outside these ringroads
was accomodation both for students and for faculty; it was an ingenious
design which allowed us to live and work close together and to avoid time-
consuming travel (2).

(2) UWI from the air. The long main drive leads to the first ring-road, housing the Faculty of Arts. Behind is the second ring-road, with the hospital in the middle of it, and left of the main drive are the buildings of the Faculty of Natural Sciences.

The History Department lay in the second ring-road, close to both the University Library and the Registry, or administrative center. Its head was then Douglas Hall, a Jamaican who had been a foremost sprinter at school (Jamaica College) and had served in the Canadian army in Italy at the battle of Anzio, about which he later taught a course. He combined a remarkable West Indian flair (he was a wonderful dancer) with an Anglo sense of efficiency. Douglas and his wife and five children lived in the former commandant's house, which was the scene of many lively departmental parties. My other colleagues had mostly trained in the United Kingdom, at such universities as Cambridge, Edinburgh and St Andrews. Thus, we taught our charges – perhaps without really thinking about it – through the tutorial system, which involved both lectures and small weekly classes at which the students would read and defend their essays.

Students would then write a series of three-hour examinations at the end of the year (in one of the large wooden structures remaining from Gibraltar Camp). This arrangement eventually came under criticism from new colleagues, trained in North America, who advocated the use of some form of "continuous assessment" and of term-papers written "at home." During my time, after some contention, there was eventually a compromise between these two systems; of course, economic considerations also tended towards a dilution of the pure tutorial system, however intellectually effective it may have been. Students always find it hard to put essays in on time, and sometimes come up with ingenious excuses. I particularly enjoyed one offered by a student who was a fine long-jumper. "Doc," he said, "have patience; I have almost finished marking out my run-up."

There was no question of "instructor's autonomy" at UWI. We agreed together on the syllabus for each course and set its examination-paper together. All examination-papers were marked anonymously by at least two markers; this system was time-intensive and required us to work a full day every day. We were rather astonished when professors came from North America and posted "office hours" on their doors... Each term we posted private comments on the progress of our students, and these could be remarkably frank. I remember that Keith Laurence (Trinidad and Clare College, Cambridge) once observed that a certain student "seems rather slow, but he has not done enough work for me to be sure of it." The Department also contained Edward Brathwaite, who wrote an excellent and very original book called *The Development of Creole Society in Jamaica* (Oxford 1971) and was one of the leading West Indian poets of his generation.

This generation of West Indian scholars felt with reason that they were opening up new fields in such areas as natural product chemistry and high-altitude physics; the same was true of historical and literary studies. I was able to continue my work on French history but was also more and more drawn into the study of Jamaican history. Everywhere you looked, the past loudly spoke, in the way people dressed and talked, in the tools that they used, in the food that they ate and so on, not least in the way that slavery manifestly continued its baleful influence. There was even a remote but direct contact with the seventeenth century, for while we were in Jamaica a plantation-owner descended directly from one of the regicides of king Charles I (executed in 1649) died.

Taking up a rather obscure aspect of this all-surrounding history, I worked on the remains of the British fortifications, often to be found in the bush by Kingston (3).

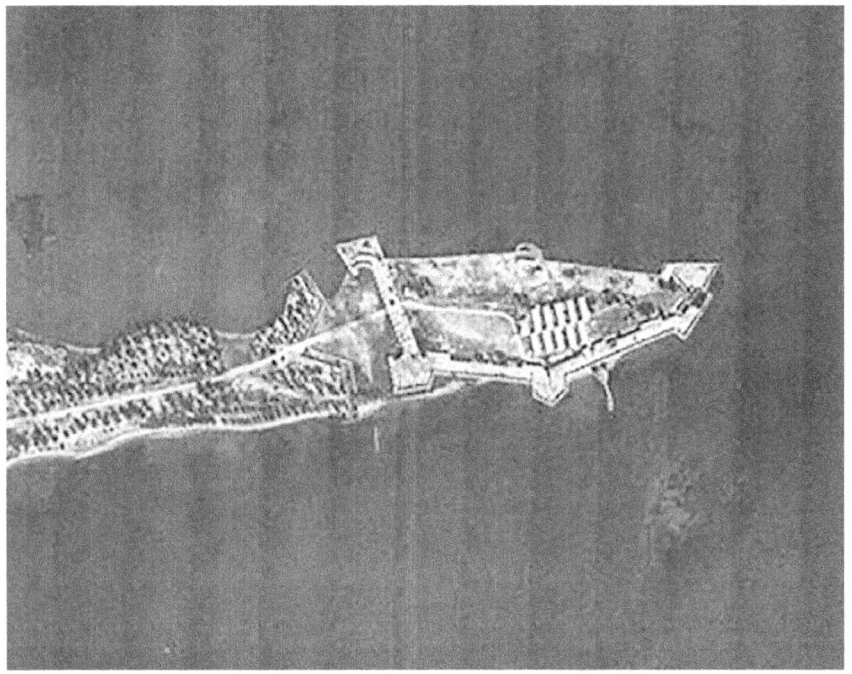

(3) Aerial view of Fort Augusta, in Kingston Harbour, about 1964. This fort, on which work began in 1740, is an astonishing example of eighteenth-century engineering. To house the 80 heavy guns, great numbers of palmetto logs had to be driven deep into the soil.

This led to many field-trips and eventually to *The Fortifications of Kingston* (Kingston, 1971) and then to *The Fortifications of Jamaica* (Kingston, 2009). These field-trips were often made with colleagues from other disciplines – geologists, orthopedic surgeons and so forth – for there was a remarkable feeling that we were all working on a common enterprise. One of my frequent companions was Mike Ashcroft, epidemiologist from the Medical Research Council and expert on sickle cell anemia. He had served in the Royal Army Medical Corps, and once, after putting a dressing on a gash that I had given myself on a field-trip, he remarked that this dressing must be a survival from his time in Korea.

In accordance with our interdisciplinary spirit, I always attended the yearly symposium on natural product chemistry, and eventually made some suggestions based on seventeenth-century texts. As Andrea Stuart, daughter of a professor of medicine, put it many years later, her father (and I) "was part of a coterie of academics who were absorbed in this pioneering project of bringing higher education to a region that previously had none. They were an idealistic and heterogenous group drawn from across the world; our neighbourhood included Indians, Africans, Europeans and Jews, as well as every possible variety of West Indian. There was an unspoken utopianism underpinning the whole enterprise. The 1960s were beckoning and everyone (or almost everyone) hoped that our little united nations were the world of the future".

This rather heady atmosphere translated into a frenetic social life. In our first years, before we had more children and became poorer, we were likely to go out for dinner on many nights of the week. Our female West Indian colleagues, in particular, prided themselves on their mastery of regional cooking, and on their knowledge of the often-arcane vegetables and fruits that they used. Sometimes we danced after dinner, and the atmosphere was, perhaps, something like what one has read of planter Kenya. So, one professor of medicine left his wife and married the wife of a local planter. Luckily the planter squared the circle by marrying the abandoned wife; they all seemed quite happy. Other such generally temporary exchanges seemed fairly common.

In its earliest years, the University enjoyed a considerable prestige within Jamaican society. For instance, the Canadian biscuit tycoon Garfield Weston, owner of a handsome estate on the North coast, for some years made some of its villas available to university staff. There was also an easy confidence that with many experts now on the doorstep, so to speak, problems in Jamaican industry and agriculture would be more easily solved. If some of these hopes were eventually disappointed, the standing of members of the University long remained high; it was unusual for a "UC doc" (a doctor from the University Hospital, as we all seemed to be to the man in the street) to be robbed, except by accident.

The University provided housing for its members, and Pat and I lived at first in a little bungalow and then, after the birth of Claire in 1968, in a larger two-storey house (4 and 5). This had been exceptionally well designed by the Steward of Estates and caught the breezes so skillfully that we never needed air conditioning; it also had a garden big enough for a cricket net for batting practice. College Common was an ideal place to bring up children, for it was a safe place with an abundance of friends in the other houses. The young Jamaican friends of our boys were particularly skillful in inventing nicknames; thus Mark, a stocky little blond, became "Deutschmark."

(4) Our first house, at University Close. It is a conventional concrete box; Dallas Mountain is in the background.

Running this establishment was Pat's job, and involved a great deal of planning, cooking, shopping and driving. She generally had a student-lodger to look after as well as the children and had to learn to manage a gardener and some sort of household helper. As she was also secretary of the Women's Club, designed to help newcomers and to take part in events like royal visits, she was always busy. She also had some entertaining adventures on the road. Returning one day when the Mona Road was deeply flooded, she impetuously drove through a deep pool. Our Humber Super Snipe was equal to it, but as she emerged, a group of Jamaican truck-drivers on the far bank began beating on the doors of their vehicles, one of them shouting, "See the little white gal go." Another time she sped away from a local garage in time to avoid a robbery that was in progress.

(5) Our house at 24 College Common. This house, cunningly designed by the University's maintenance department, made much use of louvres ("jalousies" like the set at the top left) to catch the breeze, so that we never needed air-conditioning.

We were very warmly received by Jamaican society. The Jamaican Historical Society was quick to invite us on its activities, which involved not only lectures but many field-trips. We got to know not only the island's resident historians, like H.P. Jacobs and S.A.G. Taylor, but also Society members like Cecil Langford, Commissioner of Lands with a huge knowledge of land-holdings, George Lechler, construction engineer who had worked at many sites, Valerie Facey of The Mill Press, and Tony Gambrill, actor, author and publicity-man. In fact, I soon became editor of *The Jamaican Historical Review*, a post that I kept for all my time in the island, and also was taken into the Jamaica National Trust Commission, under the direction of Pansy Hart (6 and 7).

(6) Prince Philip greeting members of the Jamaica National Trust
Commission at Port Royal in 1975. Our chairman, the novelist
Vic Reid, is on the left; the Prince was in good form.

(7) Our invitation to the reception at King's House on this occasion.

I began an inventory of Jamaican historic buildings for the National Trust, but, alas, was able to publish only the first volume, for the parish of Saint Thomas. I did, though, set up a little museum in Fort Charles at Port Royal, and this survived for many years; it may yet. I also came to understand some of the problems of historic preservation in Jamaica. Researching an early fort by a housing estate called "Harbour View," I was directed to one of the seven Matalon brothers, mighty developers from the Levant. He remembered my little fort well; as he put it, "first I blast it, then I 'doze it."

National Trust business also led me to an encounter with the Governor-General in his splendid King's House. Having been sent there in order to pick up a historical painting that needed repair, I was lurking in the Humber with Claire under a banyan tree, waiting for the aide-de-camp to show up. It was pelting with rain, and Sir Florizel Glasspole did not think that we were comfortable in the car. So, he invited us in and fed us a delicious tea, before giving us the picture for restoration.

The University had various occasions to which our friends could be invited. The grandest of these was when we had a visit from princess Alice (our Chancellor, and a great hit with rich people on the North Coast) or even from the Queen and the Duke of Edinburgh. For these occasions Pat and I dressed in our finest (8 and 9); every year there was also a splendid graduation ceremony, at which guests like Adlai Stevenson spoke, and the band of the Jamaican Defence Force, in their wonderful zouave uniforms, inspired by Queen Victoria, played an astonishing variety of music, beginning with the Academic Festival Overture and ending, sometimes, with some local dance-tune.

(8) Pat is ready to greet the Queen; note our faithful Morris station-wagon.

(9) At the reception; having lost my Cambridge medieval doctoral hat, I had a fresh one made from memory by a Jamaican tailor more used to outfitting Rastafarians.

There were also periodic receptions given by the Vice-Chancellor in his lovely garden on Long Mountain. At one of these Pat and I, seeing a slightly forlorn young man by himself, chatted him up and discovered that he was the new Australian ambassador, come at a time when there was a plan for bauxite, produced by both Australia and Jamaica, to become the commodity of an OPEC-like cartel. This plan came to nothing, but we were now launched into the diplomatic circuit, when the Australian ambassador invited us to his embassy. On that occasion the JDF band played "Waltzing Matilda," a wonderful anthem which reduced one of our Australian friends, a local teacher, to a flood of nostalgic tears. We became a fixture on the diplomatic circuit, visiting in turn the Belgians, the British, the French, the Germans, the Guyanese, the South Koreans, the Spaniards and the Germans. It was a touching experience, to stand in the elegant gardens of the French Embassy, and to hear the band of the JDF play the *Marseillaise*. By the late 1970s, moreover, our family was often short of food, so that these receptions were doubly welcome, since we might carry away some morsels.

Often the diplomats would come on field-trips of the Jamaican Historical Society, which gave them a chance not only to see the island's sites, but also to meet local people. Sometimes a junior diplomat would come and have tea with us on College Common. Once the young German *chargé d'affaires* was sitting on our verandah when Claire suddenly appeared, swinging through the air from the bars of our pergola, which held a most beautiful and scented vine (10). Landing in front of the startled German, she used the only German phrase that I had taught the children, from my days in the Army: "Hände hoch, oder ich schiesse" she said ("Hands up or I'll shoot"). Our guest appeared to take it well.

(10) Claire comes down one of the posts on the verandah;
Mark admires the tropical vegetation.

For part of our stay the US Ambassador was Sumner Gerard, former senator from Montana, appointed, as he put it in his spicy way, "by that bastard Nixon." A prewar Cambridge man, he was particularly interested in Jamaica's historical sites, and sometimes I would make up a package of early maps and plans of sites near the sea, so that we could go there in his substantial yacht, and rummage about in the bush. On one occasion we went to a site in Clarendon, close to a former US airfield. As we sat in the shade having a Red Stripe (the local beer, now widely sold in the world) or two, the ambassador was approached by a local youth, who enquired if he would like to buy in on an imminent shipment of ganja (marijuana) by air. Sumner remained silent, but I imagine that the youth must have noticed the pearl-handled revolver stuck in his waistband; nothing more was said. On our way back to Port Royal at night, we would use the diesel to speed through reef-rich waters, my astonished introduction to modern sonar aids. When Sumner was leaving in April 1977 he wrote me a rather charming letter, which reveals his dismay at the state of the island (11).

Kingston, April 12, 1977

Professor David J. Buisseret
24 College Common
Kingston 7

Dear David:

I am returning herewith your outboard engine. I do not know what Nick did to it but I hope it runs better.

I would like to take this opportunity to thank you for the various projects you came up with that we were able to fuss with together, and I am only sorry that circumstances were such that more time could not have been devoted to such intelligent enterprises. I do hope that things go well with you and your family and that in some happier time or place we will meet again.

Every best wish and kindest personal regards.

Most sincerely,

Sumner Gerard
American Ambassador

P.S.: Regretfully I have been unable to locate in the confusion of leaving any Port Morant photographs. SG

(11).

Another world which now opened up was that of the local Catholic community. As in many of the "British" West Indies, the Jesuits and Ursulines had been very active in operating excellent high schools, and the result was that many leaders in the local professions were Catholic, including Alexander Bustamante, the explosive and highly charismatic Prime Minister. Many stories accreted around Bustamante. The one I liked best concerned the allocation of a certain piece of land, wanted by both a developer and by one of the societies of Catholic sisters. "Busta" had a quick solution: "give that land to the sister-dem," he said, and so it was done. I soon decided that I needed to found a conference of the Saint Vincent de Paul Society (for helping the poor) at the University Catholic Chaplaincy, and so first met Paul Levy, Vincentian and Duke Street lawyer with an astonishing facility for raising money for useful causes. He and his wife Angela, with children the age of ours, became lifelong friends (12).

(12) Paul Levy and Kim Laurence, godparents, at
Claire's christening at Aquinas Centre.

Our situation was in some ways advantageous, for the local embassy supplied us with a good deal of USAid, in the form of bulk shipments of substances like dried milk and bulgur wheat; all we had to do was to break the stuff down and distribute it. Many students came to help, and we eventually were often fifteen or so. Our visits, two of us at a time, rarely encountered much hostility. But I see from one diary entry that they could be a little dicey: "When we visited today, the young Rastas by Icilda Smith were exceptionally lively and kept calling 'Fire, fire.' I replied as usual with 'peace and love,' watching the one with the machete."

We also needed money, and I see from the diary for 1976 that sometimes I turned preacher, talking to congregations like this:

Sisters and brothers [echoes of de Gaulle, who always said "Françaises, Français"]

> I well remember how when I was small my church would be visited every so often by thin-looking priests who would appeal for some cause dear to them. Sometimes it was for the diocesan orphanage, sometimes for a mission somewhere; you never knew. What I can remember is a certain sinking feeling as we saw a fresh appeal coming.

> So you have all my sympathy in having to listen to yet another appeal for the SVP. This time I should like to tell you of a recent and typical case. Two brothers of the Aquinas Centre Conference visiting an old lady were called by a neighbour to see two children. A girl of three and a little boy of eighteen months were all alone without food in a shack. Their mother had gone to UCH (the University Hospital) to have another child, and the father was not about. What to do?

> Thanks in part to your previous generosity, the brothers were able at once to give a neighbour some food for the children, and since then visit them and their mother weekly with milk and food. Not much, you may say, and yet perhaps enough to help these children to develop into more or less normal adults. Without your aid in the past, the fifteen or so sisters and brothers could

never intervene in this way. If you think it is worthwhile, please give us something again, so that we can continue to help those who cannot help themselves. Thanks.

Our friendship with Paul and Angela drew us into a range of Jamaican society. We enjoyed many supper-parties, always amused by the way in which by the end of the evening the men would be at one end of the verandah, talking cricket, while the women would be at the other, talking about their children. We heard many good stories, of which one must suffice. Anxious to grow some Brussels sprouts, more or less unknown on the island, Paul had been nourishing a row of these plants under a sprinkler. They were coming on well, but one day when Paul came home from the office, he found them rooted up. Aghast, he asked his gardener what had happened. "Massa Levy," said Prince, "dem lickle cabbage never gwin grow." Prince was a very treasure-house of anecdotes and pithy sayings. Asked if he had any children, he replied that "me [s]prinkle dem all over town."

As time went by, I became more and more caught up in Jamaican history, so that when our three-year contract came to an end, we did not think of returning; nor was I tempted by various offers from universities in the United States. In fact, I was fast becoming creolized, as the phrase goes, so that on one of our visits back to England one of my former teachers at Woodbridge enquired of me: "gone bush, have you, Buisseret?"

One theme which clearly needed tackling was the history of Port Royal (13). This little town on a spit in Kingston Harbour had in the seventeenth century been the rival of Boston, until the disastrous earthquake of 1692, which plunged much of it into the sea. I found a collaborator in Michael Pawson, accountant for the Jamaica Omnibus Company and skilled diver, and we worked together on our history of Port Royal, published by Oxford University Press in 1974 (with a revised and enlarged edition in 2000). In general, we tried to demonstrate that the sources for Port Royal's history, both in Jamaica and in England, were exceptionally rich, contrary to the received wisdom. We also tried make the point that Port Royal was no more "wicked" than other seaports of the time, and indeed that it closely resembled many English towns of the period in its municipal arrangements (except for its great variety of religious congregations, Anglican, Catholic and Jewish). But this attempt at revisionism fell flat, in the face of writers' desire to show that the earthquake was the reward for Port Royal wickedness; as Lord Hailes put it in 1770, "as fast as the cobwebs of fictitious history are brushed away, they will be replaced."

(13) Aerial photograph of the harbour of Kingston, seen on the left. In the middle is the airport once known as "Palisadoes" and now "Michael Manley;" behind it is the little runway made by the Fleet Arm during the Second World War. At the bottom is Port Royal, highly vulnerable on its exposed and unstable spit.

The University was generous in supporting my original work on French history; thus, after a long leave in 1966-7 I was able to publish *Sully* in 1968, with the shortcomings that I have already mentioned, and in 1972 Bernard Barbiche and I were delighted that our first volume of the memoirs of Sully received a substantial prize from the *Institut de France* (14).

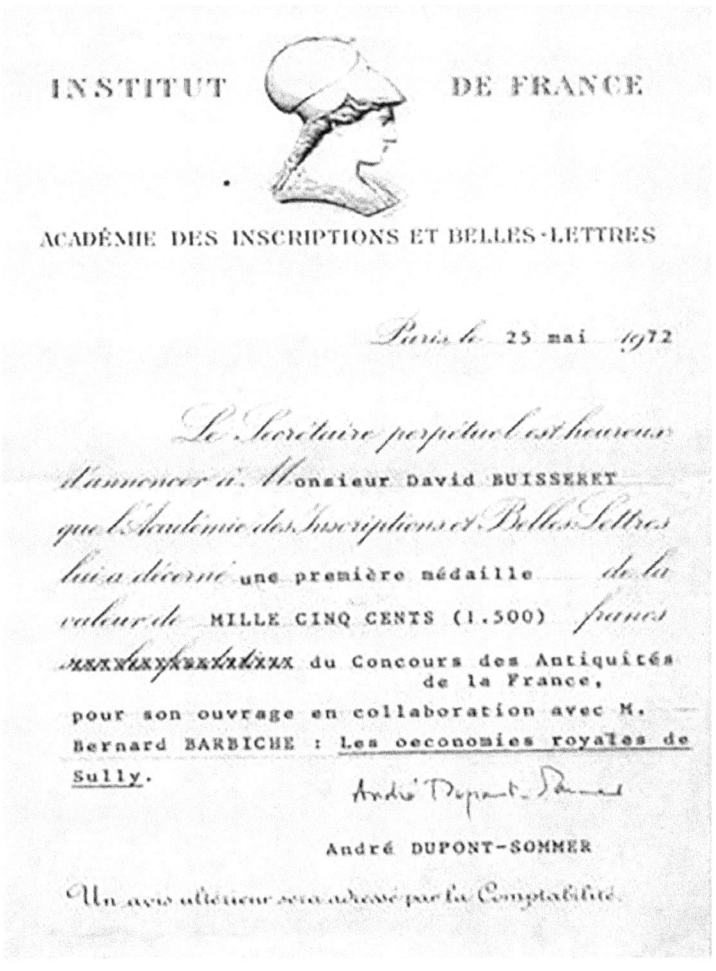

(14) This letter, delightfully archaic in appearance, let Bernard Barbiche and me know that our first volume of the memoirs of Sully had won a substantial prize.

However, it was not easy to ride two historical horses at the same time, and having been commissioned to write on the French Wars of Religion, I succeeded only in producing *Huguenots and Papists,* something of a fizzle.

Our journeys back to Europe for this work were delights in themselves, for in those days one took a variety of ships, like the *Prins der Nederlanden*, the *Willemstad* and the *Begonia* (15). Some of them also carried cargo, for which one might stop at unexpected ports like Ponce in Puerto Rico. These were sybaritic passages, on which there was often a well-equipped nursery for the children (16).

(15) The *Begonia*, of the Spanish Transatlantic Company. She called at many interesting ports in the Spanish-speaking world.

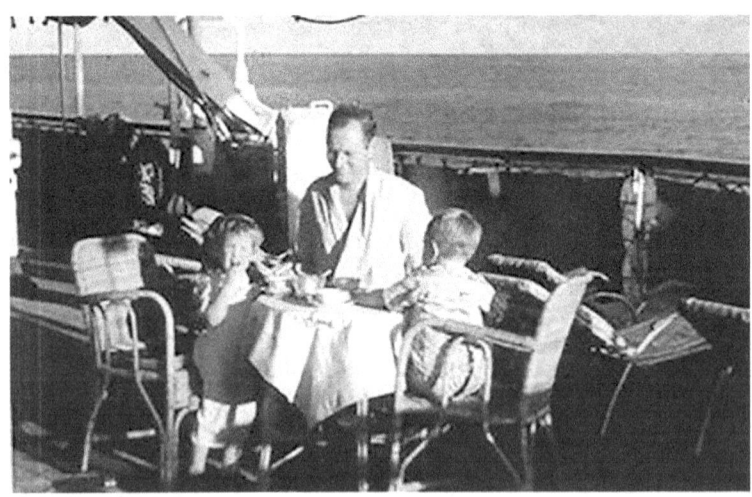

(16) Breakfast on the Dutch *Willemstad*, probably in the tropics to judge by the calm sea.

Inevitably, I got caught up in administration. I enjoyed for a long time being sub-dean (Buildings) for the Arts faculty, responsible for the maintenance of our buildings and gardens. I soon learned that in Jamaica at this time (or perhaps any time) it was not useful to write letters, or even use the telephone; it was best to stroll over to the Works Department, and after a cup of tea, and some talk about the latest cricket, get down to business. When I became Head of Department, Faculty meetings were another matter. I found it hard to stay awake in them, particularly after lunch, and see that at one such meeting I scribbled to my neighbour, a student representative, a note in which we shared our feelings (17). In general, I find the words of J.K. Galbraith on this subject full of wisdom: "Meetings are called because men seek companionship or, at a minimum, wish to escape the tedium of solitary duties. They yearn for the prestige which accrues to the men who preside over meetings, and this leads them to convoke assemblies over which they can preside. Finally, there is the meeting called not because there is business to be done, but because it is necessary to create the impression that business is being done." On the whole, in my career I have been successful in evading a great many meetings.

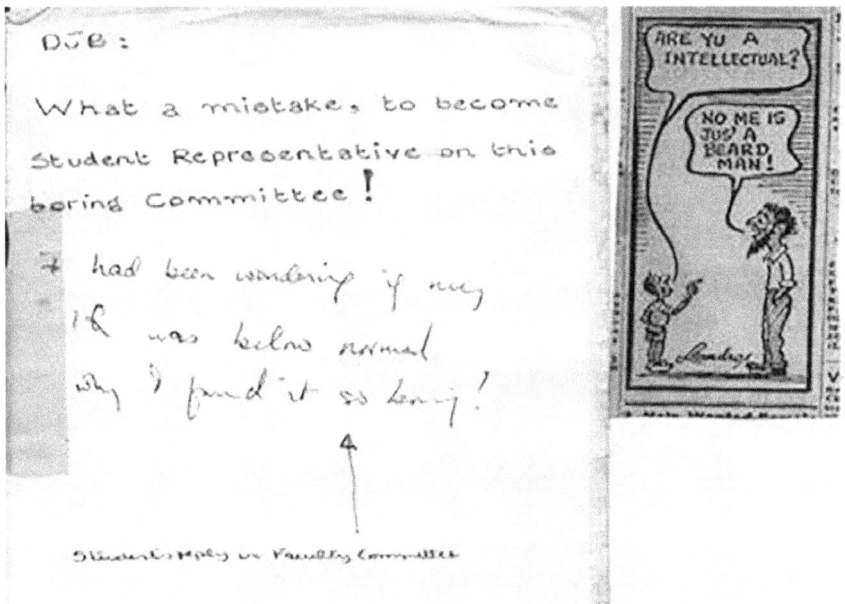

(17) An exchange of notes during a meeting of the Faculty of Arts...

Another source of meetings was our union, WIGUT, the "West Indies Group of University Teachers." As our wages insidiously sank, the union leaders persuaded their members to go on strike. I was in a quandary, because I could not imagine abandoning my classes (it was near examination-time). So I adopted a Solomonic solution; I would come to the classroom (evading the picket lines) at the usual time, and if a majority of students had turned up (and they generally did), we would have a class; if not, not. It seems to me that I was then in principle sent to Coventry (given the silent treatment), but in fact my genial colleagues could not bring themselves to do this. So the whole thing blew over; WIGUT probably did well thus to protect our interests.

(18) Pat with Hermine and Tim and Kate at Upper Albergas, Newcastle, 1965.

Jamaica offered many diversions. Perched improbably high in the hills, 4,000 feet above Mona (18), was the JDF (Jamaica Defence Force) camp at Newcastle. This had been established in the 1840s, to allow British troops some respite from the heat and diseases of the plains. It still had barracks-blocks where the JDF housed recruits for basic training, but it also had a set of empty officers' houses ("Married Quarters"), which could be rented by members of the Jamaican Civil Service and by faculty at the

University. We went up there every summer, as families in India used to go up to Simla, which Newcastle's architecture indeed rather resembled. There were wonderful walks in the surrounding hills, full of the remains of eighteenth-century coffee estates; here the children would find ancient bottles in the bush, where they had been thrown long ago by careless riders. There were also unusual birds, and superb stands of ginger-lilies, as well as tree-ferns and orchids. You could even find clumps of clover, which had presumably crossed the Atlantic with some distant English cavalry-regiment. Curiously, there were no dangerous creatures in these lovely hills (19).

(19) The Humber in the mountains near the University's house, "Bellevue."

As well as the mountains, there was the sea. I bought a little sailing-dinghy, called *Serendipity*, and we often used her to visit the cays off Kingston, either as a family or with visitors to the University. Her "Seagull" engine was notoriously fluky, but this was a safe kind of sailing; the land-breeze blew you out early in the morning, and the sea-breeze could be relied on to blow you back after lunch, sometimes faster than you expected (20). We would take a hamper out to the cay and use the driftwood to make the fire for cooking breakfast. When once or twice we got into trouble (when a fierce following sea floated the rudder out of her pintles, for instance) we could be rescued by the fishermen of Port Royal, with their Arawak-like canoes driven by powerful outboard engines. Sometimes they liked to frighten us by approaching at high speed on a collision course, and veering off only at the last minute...

(20) Pat on the beach at Gun Cay. The sea is getting up, so it is probably late morning.

The Senior Common Room, or Faculty Club, also provided sports like tennis and squash. It had a cricket team, which sometimes went to play the teams on local sugar-estates. These estates often had spacious and elegant grounds, and prided themselves on their teams, among whom there were always some fiery young bowlers, who probably also cut cane. My West Indian colleagues also prided themselves on their prowess as cricketers. This game was indeed in the process of becoming a rallying-point for West Indian nationalism; the University, the cricket team and the meteorological service were among the few survivors of the West Indies Federation (1958-1962). When a touring team came to Jamaica, the Department was closed for the opening day, and we all went down to Sabina Park. Our group was indeed a federal study in itself: Douglas Hall from Jamaica, Roy Augier (later Sir Roy) from Saint Lucia, Keith Laurence from Trinidad and Woodville Marshall from Barbados. The students had their own team, which at one time traditionally played visiting sides from places like New Zealand and Australia, to help them adjust after their long sea-voyage (21 and 22).

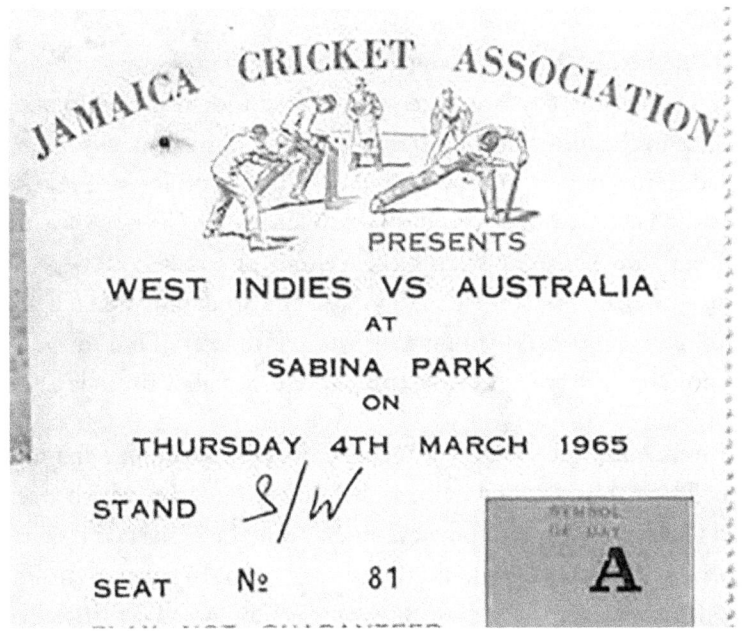

(21) Ticket-stub for the Test with Australia, 1965.

U. W. I. INTERNATIONAL CRICKET MATCH
The Officers of the University and the Guild Council
invite

Dr. & Mrs. D. Buisseret

to the University vs. Australia Cricket Match
ON THURSDAY, FEBRUARY 1, 1973
from 11.00 to 5.30 p.m.
and to Drinks at the Undercroft, 6.15 to 8.00 p.m

R.S.V.P.
Director of Sports
Phone 76661 Ext. 302

Please Bring This Card and Enter At the August Town Road Gate.

(22) Invitation to the University match with the visiting Australian test team, 1973.

At first Pat and I felt quite at home in this society of professors and students. Indeed, in our early days we once went to the Student Union to take part in a dance to the music of the Mighty Sparrow, famous calypsonian from Trinidad, notorious for his lewd rhymes ("Patsy, you look so lovely, and it is getting late..."). But as the 1960s wore on, as a reflection of what was happening elsewhere, the coming of feelings of Black Power seemed to make us unwelcome at student gatherings. The Student Union fell into the hands of a group of wild young men who played very loud music which could often be heard far and wide throughout the valley until dawn broke.

These were also the days when the Cuban government made some attempt to establish armed camps on Long Mountain, which rises just behind College Common; some evenings would be enlivened by bursts of automatic fire, as the JDF sought to dislodge them. In general, this foreign attempt to take over the Jamaican hills was bound to fail, since in most places they were inhabited not by the landless and discontented peasants of Marxist theorists, but by small farmers, much attached to their holdings.

In order to go up to Newcastle we loaded up our trusty Humber Super Snipe with equipment and food for a week or so. The Humber was a very elegant and powerful car (descendant of the wartime staff-cars), but, like so many British products in those days, lacked parts and service in Jamaica, and indeed throughout the world. I solved this problem by buying a second, more dilapidated Snipe which I kept in a corner of the garden; this I cannibalized as necessary. If the job seemed too complicated, I drove down to the Kingston yard of Mr. X, known as "Dr Peck," because he always wore a stethoscope, with which he listened to engines. Dr Peck was a real expert, who had worked building Humbers at Preston in England; he could be counted upon to intervene before I did serious damage. In those days, of course, engines were much simpler, and Mark and I (he loved to help) had no difficulty, for instance, in replacing the cylinder head liner if necessary.

The Jamaican dollar, in which we were paid, progressively declined in value against the pound, and export restrictions meant that people began to think of ingenious ways of getting their assets out; having their teeth capped with gold fillings, for instance, or taking flying lessons. Another ploy was to buy rare stamps, and this concerned me, as a member of the Jamaican Philatelic Society. One of our members was the Russian ambassador, and one of our activities was to make up booklets of stamps, which we sold among each other. I used to make such sales with the Russian ambassador, who arranged our exchanges in a rather curious way; at some precise hour, I would wait by the ring-road, and a large black Russian car would cruise up, so that we could make our exchange. I hope that at least one Western security agency has a good sharp image of this transaction...

While we were at 24 College Common (1968-80), Pat and I had two more children, Mark and Paul, to join Tim, Kate and Claire (25); both sets of parents also visited us (23 and 24).

(23) Pat's parents with us on a picnic in St. Thomas.

(24) About to leave with my parents in the Humber.

We hugely enjoyed the little boys, and once they became large enough to look after themselves (26) I thought that I would try my hand at founding a troop of Cub Scouts, since this so obviously filled a need. The troop was a great success, if rather tatterdemalion, and the wife of the vice-chancellor used to allow us to meet in a corner of her large garden, where we would light fires and cook bammies. We followed the lead of Sir Robert Baden-Powell; I became Chil the Kite, and for some years after that could easily be startled on the streets of the nearby settlement of Papine, when some huge youth would greet me with a loud "Chil, Man!"

(25) Claire and her friend Lucy Mufuka, of Zambia,
returning to 24 College Common.

(26) Mark and Paul with some villainous friends in the garden.

Alas, the combination of Cubs, the Saint Vincent de Paul Society and the headship of the Department became too much, and in the summer of 1975, I suffered a nervous breakdown. It was a curious feeling; I simply could not speak to people, let alone answer the telephone, and sought solitude at all cost. Luckily our friends rallied round; Rod and Dawn Cave found me a quiet house in the hills for a week by myself, and Angela and Paul Levy found Pat and me a lovely beach-house at Silver Sands, while they looked after our children. So I slowly pulled out of it. Curiously, at its height I thought obsessively of a street in Woodbridge called "Doric Place;" my mother had once lived there, but I did not know it at all. Throughout our days in Jamaica, too, at times of stress I would think of an idealized northern landscape; somewhere like a Baltic city that was cool, orderly and clean: Riga, maybe, or Helsinki.

Relieved of the Department, which Neville Hall took over, I soldiered on, visiting a great many Caribbean islands in the course of composing *Historic Architecture of the Caribbean* (London, 1980). This work enjoyed a modest success, particularly in its French edition. But it was a good example of a poorly-chosen theme; to take on so wide a subject would have needed a book at least four times as large. Mine simply joined two or three others that had tried to work on Caribbean architecture once-over-lightly. I should have done better to have taken on my first intention, which would have been a historical examination of the Jamaican landscape (with a good title: *"The Uncastled Landscape..."*). This idea partly emerged from a new direction that my teaching was taking. Douglas Hall had been a great enthusiast for the history of the campus, and helped me to compose *Mona Campus, An Historical Guide* (27).

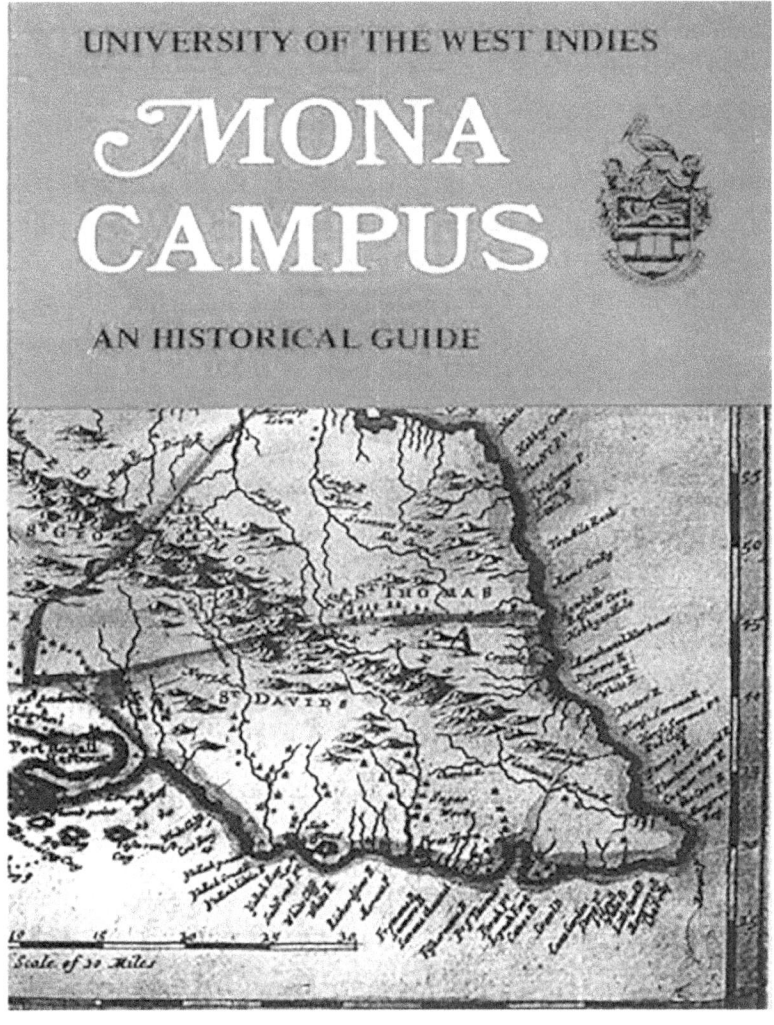

(27) The cover of the guide to the campus which I wrote about 1968. The site of the University is marked as a blue dot on this seventeenth-century map.

This led to a collaboration with Barry Higman, a very prolific and ingenious colleague from Australia. We taught a course together in which our students were encouraged to examine the Jamaican landscape. We taught them how to carry out simple plane-tabling, in order to make plans of things like the layout of estate buildings, and discussed the nature of the vegetation. We also would set the final examination requiring the students to go into the field, equipped with an eighteenth-century plan (from the Institute of Jamaica), and an aerial photograph and a section of the Colonial Survey map corresponding to the early plan; the students then had to commentate each of these documents in the light both of the others and of the actual landscape.

The students seemed to enjoy this approach, and in the late 1970s I began taking television equipment into the field, so that we could make films of students who were particularly skillful at this enterprise, perhaps to show it eventually on the local TV programme. These field-trips, for which we used our own cars, would be interrupted when our students spotted a field of succulent sugar-cane. Hastily getting out, they would return with tasty stalks on which they would chew for some time. Barry Higman carried on much the same sort of local work after I left, in 1980, and the Department eventually developed a special course in the analysis of local buildings and landscapes. This postgraduate course, for which I was for some years external examiner, produced many useful theses about Jamaican buildings and sites.

In the mid-1970s, Jamaica began to stabilize in an economic sense, though the violence was as bad as ever. Sometimes searchlight-equipped helicopters, known as "the midnight sun," would fly slowly over our gardens at night, looking for bad men hiding in the bushes. When Pat and I came back in the car, we would sometimes drive briskly onto the lawn and then dash in at one of the verandah windows, to avoid the vulnerable period when one would be walking from the open car-port to the front door. Once, too, coming home late from an evening lecture, I was chased by a carload of bad men, and only escaped by hiding deep in the pricklepear bush in the garden of our friend Ajai Mansingh. I can still hear my pursuers: "wey de lickel white man gaan?" ("where has the little white man gone?").

We felt that it was time to leave, not least because our children were reaching the age at which they could develop permanent attachments to the island; meanwhile things were getting more and more difficult for Pat, who sometimes could not find food for the children, a stressful experience. Believing that we would go back to England, in 1978 we sent Tim ahead of us, to finish his high school studies at Woodbridge School. Alas, this was a time of great retrenchment in England, and no jobs opened up for me. Then I failed to obtain what seemed like a very suitable post at Catholic University of America in Washington; things were not looking good.

Suddenly, in this dire situation a solution presented itself. When we sometimes went back to Chicago to see John and Helen, I had renewed my acquaintance with The Newberry Library, where I had held fellowships in 1965 and 1966. A particular friend there was John Tedeschi, head of Special Collections. In 1980 John was chairman of a selection committee to find a new Director of the Hermon Dunlap Smith Center for the History of Cartography. Possible candidates were few, because the history of cartography had not yet emerged as a sort of sub-discipline. John knew, though, that I had written a good deal about cartography in early modern France, and in the West Indies, and indeed that I liked to commentate my papers with my own maps. So he decided to give me a call. In principle, our telephone never worked from overseas, and often not from numbers in Jamaica. But that day it did, and a process was set in train. As my Polish mother-in-law would have said, "it was meant to be."

We distributed our rather improvised furniture to our friends – Ajai Mansingh's offspring slept for many years, and his grandchildren may sleep yet, on my sturdy cedar bed-frames – and I packed up all my books. These I put in four or five six-foot cedar boxes that I had had made. But when we then tried to lift the boxes, they were impossibly heavy, even for Jamaican movers. So, I took the books out and put them in cartons, then took the cedar boxes to the United States in order to make our new furniture there: bookcases, bedside tables and so forth. The Humber had already been sold to some cheerful Rastafarians, who used it, as my friends later observed, to run ganja into the city from St Thomas. We went for one final visit to the beach and to Newcastle (28 and 29), and then prepared for our new life in monochrome.

(28) Pat and the family on the University beach at Lyssons, about 1980.

(29) On the steps of one of the Newcastle houses for our last visit, 1980.

10

The Newberry Library, Chicago, 1980-1995

1980 was a good time to begin work in the Research and Education Division of The Newberry Library, under the direction of Richard Brown. The Library is one of a number of similar private institutions - unique to the United States - that were founded in order to collect material relating to the European discovery and settlement of the Americas. The earliest was the John Carter Brown Library in Providence; others include the James Ford Bell Library in Minneapolis and the Huntington Library in Pasadena. For many years these institutions chugged along, content to accumulate material, much of it very valuable, and to make it available to any readers who might care to use it.

The Newberry was one of the earliest of these institutions to see that its mission might also include encouraging and instructing a readership. Librarian Stanley Pargellis (1942-1962) set the movement afoot, and it was powerfully developed in the days of "Bill" Towner (1962-1986). It was then that four research centers were founded: the Family and Community History Center (1971) [now the Dr. William M. Scholl Center for American History and Culture], the Hermon Dunlap Smith Center for the History of Cartography (1971), the Center for the Study of the American Indian (1972) [now the D'Arcy McNickle Center for American Indian and Indigenous Studies], and the Renaissance Center (1979). In 1980, I became the second director of the Smith Center, when David Woodward left to take up a chair in geography at the University of Wisconsin, Madison.

The Smith Center, named after and funded by an influential Chicago insurance executive who was also a skilled historian and a longtime trustee of the Newberry, had the advantage of beginning with a substantial endowment, which it enjoyed until the original terms expired in 1991, when most of these resources were gradually absorbed into the Library's general funds. The Center also enjoyed the whole-hearted support of Bill Towner, himself a force of nature as Librarian. Bill, who had been a Mustang pilot during the Second World War, was a prominent figure in the cultural life of Chicago, making the most of his sailing-boat on the Lake, and the Library's elegant townhouse, where he and his wife Rachel loved to entertain guests.

He was closely in touch with the everyday life of the Library. I particularly remember an incident in 1965, when I had just come to the Library from Jamaica as a Summer Fellow. I was sitting on the front steps, rather sadly wondering where I would go to eat lunch, when the doors behind me flew open, and out came Bill. "Dave," he said, "shall we go and eat?" We sprang into a taxi, and sped downtown to some businessman's club, where Bill gave a speech, as I remember, criticizing the US involvement in Vietnam. Members of his audience may not all have agreed with him, but they could hardly be ignorant of his existence. He was said by some to spend money like a drunken sailor, but in his early days he was also a highly skilled fundraiser. One of his major achievements was the construction at the back of the original library of a new ten-storey brick tower, within which all the books came to be housed, under the best conditions for climate and security. One consequence of this development was that very large areas of the old building could then be devoted to study-space for scholars, and this greatly eased the pressure on accomodation. In fact, by Bill Towner's later years the Library had fostered the emergence of a community of scholars (both visiting and local) unrivalled for a while in almost any other similar library.

The Towner regime was marked by a personal and informal style. Bill was not a man of "mission statements," which have become popular and seem designed to frustrate fresh initiatives, cutting off that innovation at the fringes which often leads to fruitful ventures; I shared his dislike of this formal way of setting things up. Coming from England, I suffered from what has been called "value rigidity." Thus, it took many years before I could accept that in the United States donors to tax-free institutions like the Newberry expected still to have a say in the spending of their gifts. Indeed, I once asked one such donor if he ought not now to "butt out," having made his contribution. Perhaps I was lucky not to have been fired on the spot...

The four Centers all ran fellowship programs, organized meetings and institutes for teachers, produced publications and sometimes worked on exhibits. The original Smith endowment allowed his Center to run for many years an exceptionally lively fellowship program, drawing scholars from all over the United States, as well as from Australia, Canada, Chile, the Dominican Republic, Germany, Italy, Jamaica, Puerto Rico, Russia, Trinidad and the United Kingdom. These were early days in the study of the history of cartography, and many of our Fellows later became leading scholars in the field in their own countries (1).

(1) Lexy Postnikov, Smith Center Fellow from the Russian Academy of Sciences, outside the Library with Pat about 1983.

They also established longlasting friendships with the Center staff. Assistant Director James Akerman could give them advice on many subjects about which I was ignorant, and many Fellows well remember the help that they received from volunteer Arthur Holzheimer, who often then took them to his home in order to view his remarkable collection of maps.

At different times the Center employed Tom Willcockson, who could offer advice upon the best way to generate visual images of all kinds of material, and Tina Reithmaier, who was not only a skilful administrative assistant, responsible particularly for running summer institutes, but also pursued her own studies in local map-history.

At its height, the Center thus could offer support, help and advice to a very wide range of visiting scholars.

Tina Reithmaier, who died tragically young, was largely responsible for a series of seminars called "History on the Ground" and "Patterns on the Prairie," designed to acquaint local scholars with the region's cartographic resources. Tina had in mind the publication of a set of eight maps for each of the forty townships in the Chicago area (2), and she succeeded in shepherding to publication one of them, *Elk Grove Village and Township*, authored by David Buisseret and James Issel in 1996. Even though she did not succeed in bringing out such a publication for any other township, Tina assembled at the Library sets of images for all of them, and these still form a remarkable resource for those working in local history and genealogy.

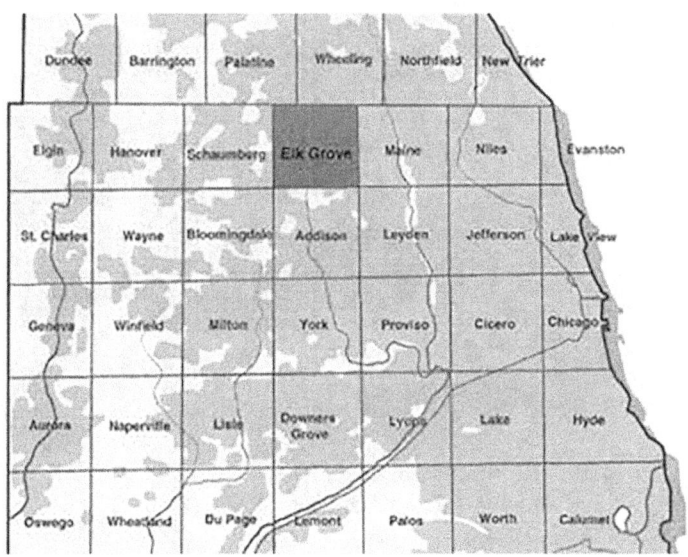

(2) Diagram of townships in the Chicago area from
Elk Grove Village and Township (1996).

The chief set of meetings sponsored by the Center was the recurrent Nebenzahl Lectures in the History of Cartography, founded and sustained by Ken and Jossie Nebenzahl in memory of their son. This series, which has reached its fiftieth anniversary, involved some complicated administration. After a distinctive and neglected theme had been chosen, something which became more and more difficult with the passage of time, lecturers had to be identified and invited, drawing on scholars from all over the world. An attractive poster would then be designed, and many of these may still be seen on the walls of sister institutions (3).

(3) Detail from the poster for *Monarchs, Ministers and Maps* (1985); note the hand on the map.

When the lecturers came to Chicago, they would be royally entertained by the Nebenzahls, and after they had given their lectures, their papers would have to be extracted from them, including any criticisms which might have been made during the sessions. With the papers in hand, and an introduction written, the collaborative volume would then be offered to the University of Chicago Press, whose readers might well offer a variety of improvements. With these taken into account, the Lectures could then pass on to publication. During the 1980s, the Nebenzahl Series dealt with the use of maps by governments (*Monarchs, Ministers and Maps,* published 1992), the mapping of countrysides on both sides of the Atlantic (*Rural Images,* 1996), and the mapping of cities in various parts of the world (*Envisioning the City,* 1998). Like my predecessor, David Woodward, I had one Series which did not reach publication, and this was the set of lectures concerning the transformation of manuscript maps into their printed, published versions. This intriguing theme, which remains untreated, could not be completed to the satisfaction of the Press's readers.

An exhibition, with accompanying catalogue, was mounted to accompany each Nebenzahl Series. Since that time, the Library has less often produced catalogues, even for elaborate and popular exhibits, and this seems a pity. The Nebenzahl endowment, together with the Smith funds, meant that we could make a record of what the Newberry held in the relevant area of cartography, and the resultant catalogue then provided a permanent record of material which scholars could expect to find at Chicago. In the years between Nebenzahl Lectures, the Center also organized exhibits on a variety of themes related to cartography, so that one new map-exhibit could be found at the Library virtually every year.

During the 1980s, these exhibitions were organized relatively informally, using the Smith funds. In 1987, for instance, for the meeting of the French Colonial Historical Society, we rapidly put together an exhibit on La Salle. As time went by, and funds ran lower, it became necessary to plan much further in advance for exhibits, and to write (slow-moving and often ponderous) proposals in order to find the funding. More recently, the Library has reverted to a more sprightly exhibit-type in the shape of exhibitions which use the Library's resources to organize material on relatively limited themes. It does seem very desirable that casual visitors can rely at any time on finding something of interest in one of the library's two exhibit-halls, as had been the case for most of the twentieth century.

We at first approached the mounting of exhibitions with what now seems absurd optimism. In 1984, for instance, Robert Karrow, curator of maps, and I were asked to mount an exhibition from Mr. Smith's fine collection of midwestern books and maps. We duly selected eighty items, wrote commentaries, set the material out in cases and published a full catalogue (4). We then took our large and beautiful exhibit-poster round to the local hotels, feeling sure that the doormen would display it prominently, and that the guests would soon be flocking to the Newberry. Alas, we soon learned that attracting visitors to the Library was more complicated than that. Occasionally exhibits were mounted in collaboration with other institutions. One of these was "Tools of Empire: Ships and Maps in the Process of Westward Expansion," mounted in 1986. It combined Newberry maps with ship-models provided by members of the Chicago Maritime Society. The exhibit attracted many viewers, but proved very complicated to organize (5).

(4) Cover for the catalogue of *Gardens of Delight* an exhibit held in 1984.

(5) Cover of the catalogue for *Tools of Empire* 1986. This
exhibit showed both maps and ship-models.

Another major type of outreach involved the organization of Summer Institutes, often for teachers at different levels. David Woodward had run one such institute on the history of cartography in the summer of 1979, and I continued this theme in 1982, 1983, 1984 and 1985, learning much about the history of cartography on the way. The approach of the Columbus Quincentenary in 1992 offered the chance for us to mount a different sort of institute, involving all the Centers in an assessment of the nature of what was beginning to be called "the encounter." The National Endowment for the Humanities ("NEH") provided funding, and for four years the Center ran changing annual institutes on "Transatlantic Encounters," very well organized by our Administrative Assistant, Tina Reithmaier. Beginning with an assessment of the English Transatlantic experience, we passed on in successive summers to that of the French, Spaniards and Portuguese.

We asked specialists to participate in the programme, but as director I had to offer the general lectures, and so to master a wide range of material, often in different languages; this proved demanding. Intellectually, the series offered the chance to make very telling cross-comparisons, and also called upon the expertise of the other Centers. Thus the McNickle Indian Center offered experts on the effect of the encounter upon indigenous societies, and the Renaissance Center offered speakers who could explain the literary consequences of the encounter in various European countries. This series of meetings attracted a large number of participants (thirty was the limit, but we often had fifty applications), and made the most of the Newberry's unique combination of material on early modern Europe, on the indigenous societies of the Americas, and on the often-catastrophic consequences of their interaction in the New World. As the participants and lecturers often came from different disciplines, there were also spirited discussions about the nature and the writing of history.

Participants were encouraged to develop their own special studies, using the Library's collections, and many of these studies took the form of six-slide sets, with titles like *Cartographic Images of the World on the Eve of the Discoveries, Missionaries in Sixteenth-Century New Spain* and *The Image of Strangers: Indian Impressions of Europeans in their Own Media.*

These slide-sets, some of which may before long be turned into electronic files, joined a whole range of publications sponsored by the Center. The most ambitious of these was a collaborative volume, whose twelve NEH-funded authors wrote about different aspects of the use of historical maps in teaching and interpreting North American history. Published by the University of Chicago Press in 1990 with the title of *From Seacharts to Satellite Images: Interpreting North American History through Maps*, this was the earliest treatment of the subject (6).

(6) Dust-jacket of *From Seacharts to Satellite Images* (University of Chicago Press, 1990), an NEH-funded manual of maps for historians. This image by George Catlin shows an early imaginary aerial view of Niagara Falls.

The abundance of Smith funds also allowed the Center to undertake a series of Occasional Publications, in a relatively informal format. Seven such volumes eventually came out, and perhaps the most useful of these was the last one, Texan scholar and Fellow Jack Jackson's annotated guide to the Karpinski Collection of early modern maps found in European archives, as far as they concerned the mapping of the region of the Gulf of Mexico. The Center at the time applied to the NEH for funds to support a more extensive guide, which would have allowed scholars studying any part of the Americas to scrutinize the Newberry's (very extensive) Karpinski material before venturing to Europe. Alas, this proposal was not accepted by the NEH, and many, though by no means all, of the maps laboriously photographed by Karpinski are now available online.

One more publication-venture which began in the Smith Center was John Long's County Boundary Project. This very extensive venture, largely funded by the NEH, migrated to the Center for Family and Community Studies (as it was then called), where it was eventually carried to triumphant completion after many years. The series of maps, covering most of the states of the Union, allowed scholars to know for any date precisely what the county-boundaries had been, thus giving geographical and statistical studies a precision that they had often hitherto lacked.

The Smith Center necessarily enjoyed close relations with the cartographic section of Library Services, and long admired the work of the curator of maps, Robert Karrow, in the compilation of his massive and authoritative *Mapmakers of the Sixteenth Century and their Maps*, published in 1993. Center staff also participated in other Library projects, such as the *Encyclopedia of Chicago History*, published by the Center for Family and Community Studies in 2004.

Coming to the Library from an academic job, in which one's day was automatically filled with lectures, tutorials and administrative duties, I was at first rather at a loss to know how to fill my days, except of course by a systematic study of the history of cartography. David Woodward took advantage of my perceived abundance of time to suggest that I take over the editorship of *Terrae Incognitae*, the journal of the Society for the History of Discoveries; I then filled this post for many years and am still its book-review editor. He also said that he was having difficulty in finding a scholar to write about early modern peninsular and colonial mapping of the Spanish Habsburg realms for the multi-volume *History of Cartography* that he was editing with Brian Harley, of the University of Wisconsin-Milwaukee. Knowing nothing about this subject, I nevertheless agreed to take it on, secure in the knowledge that the Smith travel funds would support a series of visits to the libraries and archives of Spain. In fact, they allowed me as well to visit the relevant archives in France, Germany and England, thus supporting a wide range of personal publications, like *The Mapmakers' Quest: Depicting New Worlds in Renaissance Europe*. Published in 2003 by Oxford University Press, this little book went into editions in Arabic, Spanish and Italian. My travels also allowed me to seek out scholars who might speak in the Nebenzahl Lectures.

They meant as well that I could attend the periodic meetings of the International Society for the History of Cartography, beginning with the Rome meeting of 1980. This body then asked the Smith Center to host the meeting for 1993, showing that we had reached a certain prominence in the world of historians of cartography. By then the Center was well used to organizing such reunions, and Robert Karrow compiled what he called his *Vademecum*, containing everything that a visitor needed to know about lodging, lecture-sites, transportation and so forth; it has often been useful since then. We formed a local consortium (including the Chicago Map Society and the University of Wisconsin) to mount an exhibit called *Two by Two*, which used pairs of maps to make certain points about Western cartographic history; it had an elegant catalogue (8). We also organized an evening on the lake, attended among others by Dr Helen Wallis, renowned curator of maps at the British Library (7). The public reception was held in the atrium of the new State of Illinois building, at the invitation of Jim Edgar, state governor, who was also a map collector and enthusiastic supporter.

(7) On the lake with Dr. Helen Wallis at the 1993 meeting.

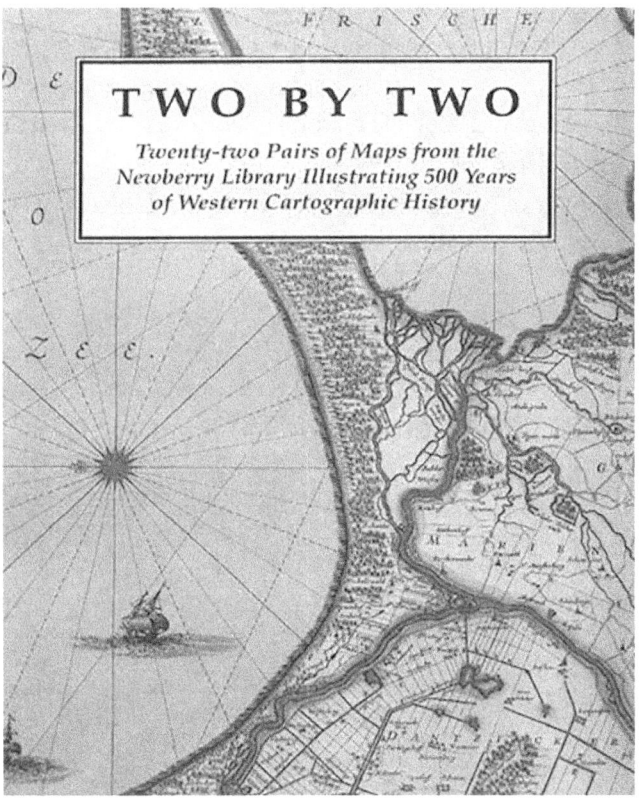

(8) Cover of the catalogue of *Two by Two* 1993. This exhibit was mounted to mark the Chicago meeting of the International Society for the History of Cartography.

With this meeting over, I felt a little as soldiers are said to feel, when after long years of training they eventually take part in some decisive engagement. It was time to think of doing something else, and to reflect on the previous sixteen years. David Woodward and I had formed a logical pair as the first two directors. David was strong in printed maps (indeed, he had his own press), in their compilation and construction, and in the early cartography of Italy. I knew little about these themes, being chiefly interested in the way that early modern European manuscript maps and their printed versions seemed to be a good way of understanding how western Europe had come to dominate the world in early modern times; I also dabbled in local history.

Our successor, Jim Akerman, carried the themes on in a chronological sense, since he developed strengths in nineteenth- and twentieth-century mapping, and in newer theories relating cartography to such fields as narrative literature and ecological studies. For my part, I now applied in 1995 to be considered for the newly-founded Garrett Chair in the History of Cartography and Southwestern Studies at the University of Texas at Arlington, and was accepted there.

11

Family life in Chicago, 1980 onwards

The decline of the Jamaican economy and of its dollar meant that our salaries bought less and less, and that saving money was out of the question. So, when we came to Chicago in 1980, we were happy to move into the house of Pat's mother Helen, who had recently been widowed. It is hard, now, to believe that we paid Helen interest at 12%, regarded as a bargain in those days. The little ranch-house has a substantial garden and lies in the suburb of Skokie ("marsh" in the local Potawatomi dialect), about twelve miles north of central Chicago. Skokie had been settled in the 1850s by truck-farmers from Germany and Luxembourg, who would send their produce to the Chicago markets down Lincoln Avenue, now one of the major diagonal roads, prominent for that reason in the chessboard pattern. Lincoln had once been a country lane, and before that a Potawatomi trail. I sang in the choir at Saint Peter's with an old German, Larry Blaumeuser, who remembered that as a little boy he had been frightened on this road riding with his father to market, since the trees, arching overhead, made it so dark.

After the Second World War the "village," as it is curiously called, became home to many Jewish families, and then in the latter half of the twentieth century it has welcomed a huge variety of other immigrants, from countries as diverse as Korea, the Philippines, Mexico and Russia. Eventually, on our street of sixteen houses we could count people born in ten different parts of the world. It had become a truly diverse community, in which many different languages could be heard.

Almost all the truck-farms had given way by 1960 to housing tracts and to a wide variety of factories making things like communications equipment (A T and T), office machines (AB Dick) and pharmaceuticals (Searle). For some years, these industries offered good jobs to graduates of the local high schools, who could count on earning enough to buy their houses and send their children to the excellent local universities, even, perhaps, to acquire a little cabin in the Northwoods. Around 1980, when we arrived, all this began to change. The work of manufacturing was more and more outsourced, at first to Mexico and then to China, and the local factories were often replaced by "box stores," selling goods generally made overseas. This had a marked effect on the local social structure, where single-earner families became relatively rare. However, Skokie did not fully feel the harmful effects of these developments, because the role of manufacturing, as a source of well-paying jobs, was to some extent replaced by the development of research laboratories, entertainment complexes and extensive medical establishments like Skokie Hospital.

The farmers from Germany and Luxembourg had been both Catholic and Lutheran, and each denomination built elegant little churches, with attached schools. We sent our youngest children, Mark (7) and Paul (5) to the local Catholic church, "Saint Pete's," while Kate and Claire went to the local public school, Niles West. This high school had high academic standards, perhaps in part because of the emphasis placed on education by the Jewish families of the 1950s. This may also account for the emergence of a well-funded local library, which continues to offer an astonishingly wide variety of programs, including much live music, as well as a fine collection of books, and draws on a wide field of patrons, many from outside Skokie.

Many of the people who settled in Skokie in the 1960s were newcomers to the United States, and were happy to cast off their former customs. For instance, they rather despised the idea of a vegetable-garden, and did not take strolls in the neighborhood, as their forebears might have done. To have a clothes-line in your backyard also seemed rather old-fashioned. Eventually, the next generation often reverted to these older customs, happily not including the internecine rivalries that in their "old countries" would have divided our now peaceable neighbors.

Machines of various kinds have often taken over what was done by hand. The mechanization of washing clothes has been a huge boon, though it is less obvious that dishes need to go in a machine. In the garden, lawns are mown, bushes are cut, and leaves and snow are now blown by polluting gas engines. These are operated by "landscape gardeners," whose week-based contracts mean that the work is carried out whether it is needed or not. This wasteful use of power is aggravated by the abundance of "security systems," which often involve a large number of quite unnecessary lights; the local police are in fact alert and efficient. Skokie has a relatively developed system of public transportation, but the scattered nature of the housing means that cars have to be widely used, a further source of noise and air-pollution. On the positive side, bicycles have lately come to be used much more widely by many different people.

The makes of the cars have greatly changed. When we arrived in 1980, the only car that we could afford was the notoriously unreliable Ford Pinto; ours, indeed, once broke down on the expressway, leaving us in a seriously dangerous situation. We followed that with a Dodge Aspen, whose only redeeming feature was its superb slant-6 engine, from Mitsubishi. Like many others, we soon switched to foreign cars; a series of VW Foxes, and then a Mitsubishi Diamante wagon (made in Australia) followed by Subarus (made in Indiana and Japan). The major Detroit manufacturers were long afflicted by the kind of sclerotic thinking found in all large organizations. Most, unlike their English counterparts, seem largely to have recovered, an astonishing revival.

We used our various cars not only for business, but also for camping trips in the summer, towing all our equipment on a flat Korean-made trailer. In the early 1980s, we generally went to the excellent state camp-grounds in Wisconsin, whether in Door County on Lake Michigan, or further north to the camps on the southern shore of Lake Superior. We often encountered American Indian communities and realized from their surnames that these were in effect *métis*, Franco-Indians. In the little Catholic church near Hayward, for instance, on Lake Court-Oreille in Wisconsin, the clearly "Indian" parishioners had names that I recognized from seventeenth-century France. As time went by, Mark and Paul became impatient with these tamer sites, and wanted to go further and further north. So, we discovered the wonderful Canadian sites on the north shore of Lake Superior, where moose might pass right by your tent, and loons could generally be heard on the lakes with their plaintive cry. On top of our other equipment, and protecting it from rain, we carried a little sailing-boat called a Snark, and this proved ideal for the lakes, even including Lake Superior on calm days (1).

(1) Mark and Paul sailing the Snark on Lake Huron about 1989.

There were other interesting sites, closer to home. Every Christmas we went to cut a tree on the farm run by the Benedictine Military School (perhaps an unhappy combination of adjectives?) out to the west, near the Fox River, an area early settled by Europeans in the 1830s. This farm lies close by Fermilab, site of a huge circular linear accelerator (several miles round) run by the Department of Energy. In Fermilalab's central building we could hear more or less uncomprehendingly about such things as the subatomic particles, quarks and bosons; we could also admire a fine collection of Potawatomi artefacts found on the site and check on the progress of their herd of buffalo (2).

(2) Pat with Mark and Paul at Fermilab around Christmas of 1984.

Another interesting local site for us was the town of Pullman, a few miles to the south. Here the enterprising George Pullman had manufactured the famous "Pullman cars," the last word in passenger comfort on nineteenth-century railways in the United States. Pullman built a model village for his workers, and this still survives (3). Alas, his excessive "paternalism" eventually led to a crippling strike.

(3) Pat and her mother on a walk at Pullman village, about 1985, with the workers' nineteenth-century model houses in the background.

During the 1980s, we had to think about the further education of the children. Timothy was now in Suffolk, at Woodbridge School, and when he graduated from there, he entered the Royal Navy, training first at the Royal Naval College, Dartmouth, and then at the naval engineering college at Manadon, outside Plymouth in Devon (where his great-grandfather had been the borough engineer, around 1900) (4).

(4) Tim at his Manadon graduation, with Pat and Kate, about 1985.

Kate went to Niles West, and shortly afterwards joined the Illinois National Guard, where she trained in the blistering heat of Texas as a "medtech," or nurse (5). Claire also went to Niles West, and then to Loyola University in Chicago, where she read history and literature, and attended Loyola's Center in Rome for one delicious semester in 1988.

(5) Kate on leave from her training with the Illinois National Guard, about 1985.

After "Saint Pete's," Mark and Paul also went to Niles West. We should then have liked to send Mark to the University of Chicago, which offered a combination of subjects in the arts and sciences for which he would have been a good candidate. But this university was already prohibitively expensive, and so he went to the University of Illinois at Champaign-Urbana, entering their excellent program in chemical engineering. Studying petroleum engineering, he spent a term at the University of Swansea in Wales, and this allowed him to visit his English relatives in Suffolk.

That left Paul, who spared us the high fees of the United States by winning a place at Queen's University in Ontario, Canada. We hugely enjoyed driving him to Kingston, at the entrance to the Saint Lawrence River, taking a variety of routes alongside the Great Lakes. Paul read geology, for which Queen's has long been famed, and had no difficulty afterwards in finding a job as an exploration geologist.

After their various graduations, the children entered appropriate fields, though they all eventually switched professions, as seems typical of our times. After leaving Manadon, Tim also left the Royal Navy, which seemed to be in a constant process of contraction, and went to study information technology at the University of Manchester. There he met Yura Vassileva of Bulgaria, on a postgraduate course in architecture, and in 1993 they were married (6).

(6) The marriage of Tim and Mira at the Russian
Church of Saint Nicholas, Sofia, 1993.

Kate left the National Guard after five years, serving for part of that time with the refueling wing based at O'Hare, and flying with one of their aircraft as it refueled the Guard's fighters. After various jobs she found her vocation as driver of school buses, which has made her many friends over the years. Claire taught for a while and worked as office manager for the Kellogg School of Business at Northwestern University. Then she met Tom Nachbar, who had read history at the University of Illinois, and had entered business, working for firms like Arthur Anderson and Hughes Electronics. Like our children, Tom also switched professions, reading law very successfully, first at Tulane University and then at the University of Chicago. Tom and Claire were married at Saint Peter's Church in 1996 (7).

(7) Claire arriving for her marriage at Saint Peter's in 1996 in company with her uncle Kit; her friend Anna Minkov follows.

When he left the University of Illinois, Mark joined Universal Oil Products, at first as a storekeeper and then as one of their engineers. This firm was famous for the contribution that it had made to the Second World War, by manufacturing an exceptionally effective fuel for aircraft engines. Universal Oil had many patents for the efficient operation of refineries, and Mark joined the young engineers who were sent all over the world to put these procedures into practice. He worked in many hot and often hazardous countries: India, Pakistan, Turkey, Mexico, Spain and so forth. While on this work he met a fellow engineer, Louise Dane, who had recently graduated from Texas A and M University. They served together in Mexico and Turkey, and eventually decided to leave their peripatetic life, Mark retraining as a lawyer, and Louise as an actuary. They married in 2000 (8), and for a while lived in a charming little house close by Lake Michigan, in Evanston. Here two children were born, Rafe and Meghan; Mark eventually took his skills as a patent lawyer to work with the British-based firm Smith and Nephew in Memphis, Tennessee. Meanwhile Tom had become a professor of law at the University of Virginia, so that they live at Charlottesville with their four children: James, Amelia, Alex and Jack.

(8) Mark and Louise after their wedding in the Methodist church at Texarkana in 2000.

Paul, too, at first followed a travelling life, working for some years in Alaska, where he lived in many remote parts, checking the local geology for gold-bearing rock. He was employed by the mining giant Newmont, and would gather sample cores in the summer, which he would then analyze during the following winter (9).

(9) Paul outside his tent in Alaska, about 1998.

Eventually tiring of this remote life, he resettled in Colorado, intending to qualify as a physician's assistant. However, the physician at the clinic in Aspen where he now worked encouraged him to train instead as a doctor. So, he attended the University of Colorado's School of Health, qualifying in 2005 and then working as a general practitioner for Kaiser Permanente in Denver.

During their years growing up in Skokie, the children sometimes came with Pat and me during the summer to Europe, partly to visit their grandparents in Woodbridge. Once Ralph and Maidie crossed the Atlantic to see us in Skokie; they greatly enjoyed picnics by our various lakes (10).

(10) Kate with her grandfather by a lake in Illinois, 1982.

Ralph died in 1984, but for many years my mother remained fairly hale, able to come out with us and enjoy a pub lunch (11). We took her each summer for a holiday as far as she could manage; at first to the Isle of Wight, then for some years to Southwold, and finally just on local expeditions from Woodbridge. She had found a very congenial lodging in one room of the Old Court House, where several other single ladies lived. This elegant house had been the quarters for the judge on circuit, and when she lived there, she happily used an electric scooter to get around Woodbridge and keep up with her old friends; she died in 2003. On our last visit to Woodbridge, we were sad to see that the Old Court House had been transformed into a set of luxury apartments. In fact, during our visits to England we had felt less and less attuned to the new society which emerged during the late 1960s. The Angry Young Men and their culture of complaint seemed to have given rise to a generally self-indulgent society, in which drunkenness, drug-taking and lavish emotional display had become commonplace; perhaps we were better off out of it.

(11) Maidie enjoying lunch with Pat at the Red Lion, Martlesham, about 1995.

I often used the summer to visit archives in Spain, France and Germany. In 1988, when Claire had finished her time at the Loyola Center in Rome, she came with me on a research trip to France, camping with minimum equipment carried in a little Citroën (12). When Mark came with us on vacation, he always carried a fishing-rod, and at Cambridge in 1985 caught a pike in the River Cam (13). During one of our stays at Woodbridge, Paul sailed our model yacht in the yacht-pond, then a very common feature of English towns (14). All the children enjoyed our stays on the Isle of Wight, with its wonderful walks along the downs, where succulent blackberries might be found.

(12) Claire at our campsite outside Arles, in southern France, in 1988.

(13) Mark with the pike that he caught in the River Cam at Cambridge in 1985.

(14) Paul sailing our model yacht on the yacht-pond at Woodbridge, about 1984.

Our house in Skokie had been too small for four children (Tim was already in England when we moved there), but then, with only Kate still at home, it became amply large for the three of us. We toyed for some years with the idea of moving, but eventually decided that Skokie had the great advantages of easy access to the lake and to the Newberry, as well as to O'Hare airfield. Meanwhile the village was again changing its character, as with the collapse of the Soviet Union more immigrants came from Russia and the former satellites. Many brought valuable skills, but some also brought money that needed to be laundered. So to our astonishment we began to see entirely improbable businesses emerging, as well as huge new houses that rarely seemed fully occupied. The Skokie of the German truck-farmers, of which we had caught echoes in 1960, had finally disappeared.

For many years, we succeeded in getting back occasionally to Jamaica, for me to work and so that we could see old friends. In Skokie there was now a Jamaican restaurant, where we could encounter some of the tastes and smells of the tropics and catch up on some local news. Sometimes such memories came from even further back; thus, at a barbecue in a local park the cook used a certain cooking-fuel. It was the same one that our cooks had used at Gebel Maryam, and I was instantly transported back to that sandy scene.

12

The University of Texas at Arlington, 1995-2006

The University of Texas at Austin has a number of more or less subsidiary campuses, at places like Arlington, Dallas, San Antonio and El Paso. UT Arlington ("UTA") had long been the special preserve of Jenkins Garrett, a Fort Worth lawyer who was also for some time a member of the Board of Regents, as well as a keen local historian. Jenkins and his wife Virginia were lifelong residents of Fort Worth, who could remember its early days and such landmarks as the flight of the first B-29 (a powerful and innovative four-engine bomber) in the 1940s. When then, the Regents wished to establish at Arlington a "center of excellence" (as the phrase went) in the history of cartography, they naturally named it after the Garretts; it was for this founding chair that I had applied. Once appointed, Jenkins and Virginia kept up a lively and often jocular relationship with me. I see, for instance, that when they sent me photos of some occasion or other, Jenkins noted that they were "not very good," but that he had sent them all, "except for a few that I have saved for blackmail purposes."

Appointments to academic posts seem to be one of the few survivals of the fully democratic appointment-process in the United States, where after interviews and a presentation the Department as a whole votes on the candidates. As far as I could tell, no outside pressures or imperious deans came into play; the process was thus untypical of the present-day United States. The Department was in a process of transition. "UTA" had begun in the late nineteenth century as a local military college, whose teachers were not expected to carry out much research. This tradition was slowly giving way, after several institutional transitions, to the expectations of a modern research university (it has recently received this national ranking), but the process was slow. For instance, it proved impossible in my day to institute monthly departmental seminars, at which we all in turn could speak of our research and that of our students. Happily, that has now changed. In one way, we seemed to be doing well, because our new appointments were regularly poached by more prominent universities.

For many years the Department had sponsored the annual Webb Lectures, organized by different members of the Department, and then published in a long and distinguished series. To this series was added in the 1990s a further series of publications, generated from the periodic Garrett Lectures in the History of Cartography. These cartographic lectures were accompanied by appropriate exhibitions in Special Collections of the University Library, to which Virginia Garrett's maps had been given. Full catalogues were prepared of each of these exhibitions, by curators Kit Goodwin and then Ben Huseman, and these catalogues now offer a very good overview of the kind of material available at Arlington, chiefly of interest to historians of the southwest of the United States but extending as well into Mexico.

At the Newberry Library, I had not encountered the general run of high school graduates, since those who came there were by definition seriously interested in research. At UTA, however, apart from our history majors, we generally taught a rather low level of students, particularly from the schools of business and marketing. On the other hand, students from the well-regarded school of nursing were often a pleasure to teach.

What exactly, though, was one teaching? Clearly, one could not expect a great deal of academic work from students who often had more or less fulltime jobs, as well, often, as complicated family responsibilities. But were we meant to be teaching an "area of knowledge," or "research competence," or both? And how was this teaching to be examined? Surely not merely by multiple choice questionnaires, however useful these might be in the course of the term. Most of my students, though, were quite unable to tackle the traditional end-of-term three-hour paper, of four questions. I did persist in setting these, though the results were in general dismal; many of the students would leave the examination-room long before the time was up. To try to help, I would organize voluntary sessions in which we would write an essay together. Having identified the theme, we would work out half a dozen or so points to be made, and then ask for suggestions from the class, a sentence at a time. Once our essay was complete, I would type it up and send a copy to all those who had participated. I do not know if this was helpful, but at least it showed the students what I hoped for. Of course, among our history majors there were students who did excellent work.

The assessments which I received from the students at the end of the term were revealing in their wide fluctuation. Some wondered where the University could have found this fossil, while others enjoyed my freewheeling, textbook-free approach. At the end, my approach and belief were summarized in this way by Tony Judt: "I teach the legacy of long-dead Europeans, have little tolerance for 'self-expression' as a substitute for clarity, regard effort as a poor substitute for achievement, treat my discipline as dependent in the first instance on facts, not 'theory,' and view with skepticism much that passes for historical scholarship." Judt was a fellow dinosaur...

The Department had had a more or less random selection of research students, studying such themes as interested their supervisors. We tried to bring some coherence to this program, choosing the over-arching theme of "transatlantic encounters." The students themselves then formed a "Transatlantic Studies" group, which still survives, thrives and sponsors annual conferences. I felt at home in this program, which rather resembled the "transatlantic encounters" summer institutes that I had directed at the Newberry, leading up to the Columbus quincentenary. I also had four or five doctoral students, whose theses concerned such themes as "piracy in the Atlantic," "the origins of the *acequia* system [of water-distribution] in central America" and "the maps of the Thames School of cartographers" [1580-1660].

Another successful project was the Texas Map Society. David Woodward had founded such a society (probably the first in the world) at the Newberry in 1971, and this Chicago Map Society continues to thrive. The "CMS" holds monthly meetings for nine months of the year, relying to some degree on scholars using the Newberry's collections. This model would not have been appropriate for a society based on Arlington, which did not have the same constant flow of scholars. So the Texas Map Society meets twice a year, once at Arlington, where scholars present four or five papers around a chosen theme, and then once elsewhere in the state. The Society thus reaches enthusiasts all over the state, holding meetings at places like Alpine, Austin, Dallas, Galveston, Lubbock and San Antonio (1). These meetings, often splendidly hosted by some local member, are frequently memorable social occasions, as well as an opportunity to study the local maps.

(1) At Fort Davis, during the Texas Map Society's meeting at Alpine.

In general, I did not circulate as much as I had hoped among local supporters, as had been the case at the Newberry; perhaps my politics were not in tune with theirs. I do remember that when preparations for the war with Iraq were under way, I was asked (as a French historian) by the local TV station to explain France's "milktoast" attitude. I pointed out that the French are a logical people, who could not see the point in attacking Iraq, when the 9/11 aggressors had been mostly Saudis, directed from Afghanistan; that they have a sense of history that does not commend the idea of "preventive strikes," and that finally their own experience of "shock and awe" in 1940, called the *Blitzkrieg*, had left an indelible trace. Needless to say, this interview was not broadcast...

At UTA, I continued to edit *Terrae Incognitae*, the journal of the Society for the History of Discoveries, with the help of a succession of graduate students. About 1998, Oxford University Press, in collaboration with the Newberry Library, conceived the idea of an *Oxford Companion to World Exploration*, and asked me to edit it. The Dean of the Faculty of Arts kindly consented to my spending half of the year on this work, so that from 2000 onwards Pat and I spent the hottest months in the relative cool of Chicago. Some editors have found the work of an Oxford *Companion* taxing and long-drawn-out. However, I was very lucky in my choice of four dynamic and efficient sub-editors, who knew their fields well and knew which scholars would be reliable. When they sent in the texts with a bibliography, I would call up these books in the Newberry, and select from them appropriate illustrations, thus giving our *Companion* an unusual combination of text and highly relevant image. One or two critics eventually complained that we had not given sufficient emphasis to non-European explorers, but it was not for want of trying.

Arlington itself originated as a stop on the railway line (the "TPR", or Texas and Pacific Railroad) between Dallas and Fort Worth, where cotton was loaded from the local plantations; the University lay, indeed, on land that had been part of a cotton farm. Plate 2 shows the area in the 1860s. Arlington emerged from "Johnson's Station," a stop on the coach-route between Dallas and Fort Worth; the railroad eventually replaced this route. The unmarked river leading north by Johnson's Station to the "West Fork" (of the Trinity River) was called "Trading-house Creek," and elegantly runs through the University. Arlington greatly expanded in the 1950s, largely because General Motors then sited an assembly-plant there. Arlington's longtime mayor had been greatly impressed by the urban patterns that he saw as a student in California, and so the emergent city of eventually nearly 400,000 people followed this unfortunate example.

The old downtown, where the local farmers and their wives had shopped, was neglected, and the inhabitants of the sprawling suburbs went to do their shopping in one of the peripheral malls. There was no public transport, everything being dependent on private cars. This led to a very difficult situation for our foreign students, some of whom had to walk several hot miles in order to reach a shop. Eventually, the University's planners saw that they needed to expand its residential-halls in the direction of the old downtown, and this policy has not only resulted in some fine buildings, but has also been fruitful in encouraging a growing relationship between what used to be called "town and gown."

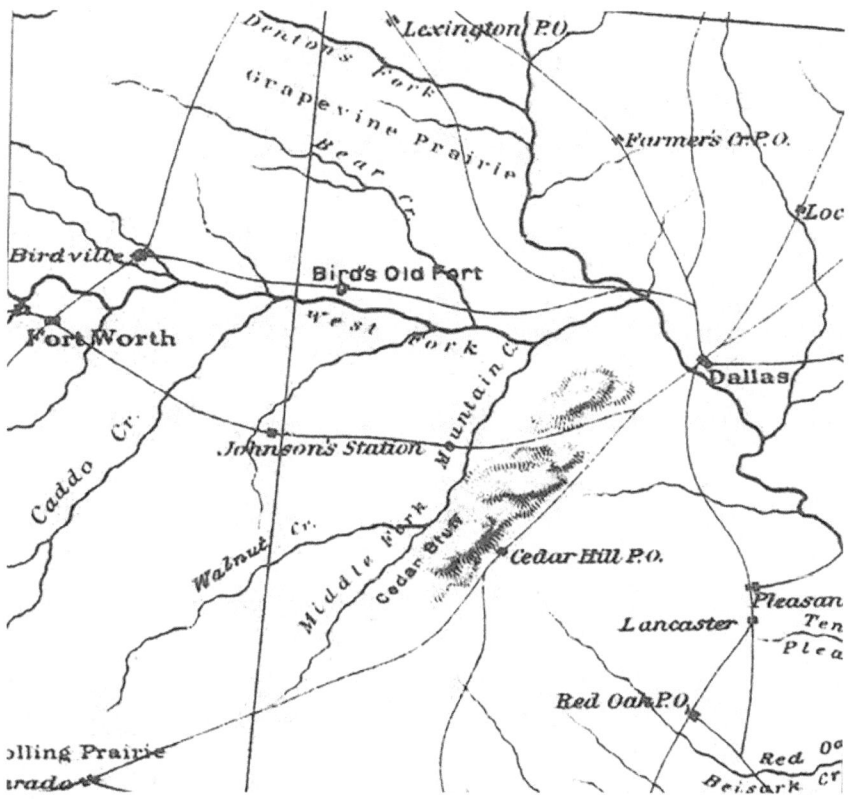

(2) Detail from the *Atlas to Accompany the Official Records of the Union and Confederate Armies, 1861-1865* (Washington, 1861).

Houses in Arlington were relatively cheap, and we found one within cycling distance of the University. It had an elegant garden, and room for two or three visitors, and lay among the band of oak-trees known as the "Cross-Timbers" (3). This remarkable natural phenomenon consists of a band of oak-trees beginning a little south of us in Texas, and then running north-east into Oklahoma. The only problem with living under the oaks was that their leaves could only be composted very slowly. The house was amply big not only for many visitors, but also for hosting student events.

(3) Our house in the oak forest at Norwood Lane, Arlington.

The climate in Arlington is trying. Pat and I would drive the 900 miles or so from Chicago in two days, stopping every hundred miles or so in Illinois, Missouri, and Oklahoma, before crossing the Red River and entering Texas. For our first few stops, we would say to ourselves that the heat was tolerable. But once we reached Oklahoma, upon leaving our air-conditioned vehicle we would wonder that people could live in this torrid climate. The fact is that for much of the year urban Texas would be unlivable without air-conditioning; tarmac is a very poor replacement for grass and trees.

The unplanned suburban nature of Arlington's townscape was also depressing to the spirit. When I first went there, I found it essential to escape each day to what remained of the countryside; I came to appreciate, in fact, the observation of Wordsworth that contact with the countryside was a positive necessity for the mental and physical wellbeing of many city-dwellers. Luckily, there was a delightful walk alongside the banks of the Trinity River, running between Fort Worth and Dallas, and a bicycle-track round part of Lake Joe Pool, fifteen miles or so to the south. This is an artificial lake, made by a huge earthen dam, and the south side of it was immune from development, since it had become Cedar Hill State Park. With one of my research students, we kept a sailing-boat on this lake, where the sailing could be lively, as Pat demonstrates (4). Texas is liberally sprinkled with such manmade lakes, some of them very large indeed, requiring nightly radio "marine forecasts." Before the creation of these bodies of water, much of the land must have been mighty hardscrabble. But prosperity often came to the most unlikely places through the discovery of oil.

(4) Pat at the helm of our boat on Lake Joe Pool.

Arlington lies between Dallas and Fort Worth, and this proximity (30 miles) of two large cities seems to defy the geographers' ideas about "central place theory," according to which cities of such size ought to emerge at a fair distance one from another. Their existence only makes sense when one realizes that while Dallas faces eastward, towards the crops of the blacklands and the piney woods, Fort Worth looks resolutely westward to the great cattle estates; both cities also came to float on oil and then natural gas.

Pat and I rarely ventured to Dallas, with its terrifying canyon of expressways. But we often went to Fort Worth, where there was a fine new concert hall called "the Bass," a remarkable museum of Western Art called "the Amon Carter," and, more surprisingly, a new art-museum known as "the Kimbell." The latter had in fifty years assembled an astonishing collection, with well-chosen examples of most of the phases of Western art. The Kimbell seemed to us the very model of an art museum; located in a fine building by Louis Kahn, it offered a permanent collection small enough for one to know it really well, as well as monthly lectures by visiting scholars, often concerning items in the permanent collection. Generally intimidated by the "blockbuster" shows of the Art Institute of Chicago, Pat and I became *habitués* of the Kimbell (5).

(5) Pat at the Kimbell Art Museum, in front of the statue by Maillol.

Pat also became a volunteer gardener at Fort Worth's elegant Botanical Garden. Once, going to pick her up there towards the end of the morning, I came upon a group of ladies, fellow-gardeners. Cheerfully, I asked them if they knew where Pat could be found. Receiving no reply, I asked again, even more jovially. "Listen, bud, we're here on release time (from the penitentiary). *** off, willya," one of them said.

When we ventured further afield, it was often to visit the little towns scattered through the ranch country to the west. These gave one a better understanding of the Texan psyche, and particularly the fondness for guns and the feeling of sturdy individual independence. At a small town like Lampasas, for instance, it was only a little over one hundred years since the Apache were still raiding, so that a handy loaded rifle was not a luxury, but essential. This applied as well to remote ranches, in the country where Pat would sometimes remark: "I sure hope we don't break down here." On these ranches it might be necessary to defend oneself, as well as treating maladies in men and beasts, and mending obdurate machinery. People living here could easily feel self-made and self-reliant, particularly if, as was sometimes the case, chance finds of oil had also made them rich.

This exaggerated notion of self-reliance makes Texas seem substantially different from the other states on the Union, a difference underscored by the fact that Texas was for a while independent (1836-1845); the Texan flag is still flown there **alongside** the Stars and Stripes. This feeling of uniqueness gives rise to many good stories. When, for instance, admiral Crowe was US ambassador in London, he was asked by an indignant Member of Parliament how the Federal government would feel, if a group appeared to be encouraging the secession of Texas, as some Irish patriots appeared to be encouraging the secession of Northern Ireland. Crowe had the perfect diplomatic answer: "Sir," he said, "you have asked the wrong man. I am from Oklahoma, and the secession of Texas has often seemed a good idea to us."

Indeed, the very appearance of the Texan landscape, divided by a variety of landholding systems, sharply distinguishes it from the states of the north. In most of these the roads and holdings largely run north-south and east-west, forming a checker-board following the provisions of the land-ordinance of 1785. Texas was then part of Mexico, and the land was often divided into irregular ranches, often on the diagonal, thus giving it a very different appearance. This difference was amusingly illustrated when the US government in the 1860s (when Texas had joined the Union) was sending out forms to people who had applied to act as postmasters in their area. These forms had maps which would allow the postmaster-general to assess the validity of various suggested sites, and they were naturally divided into the squares of the township-and-range system. Receiving one of these maps, one indignant Texas applicant replied that this was an unintelligible "yankee map," but that she had nevertheless tried to mark her position in relation to the nearest creek.

The most remarkable historical structures in the Texas countryside were the forts and missions. The forts mostly dated to the nineteenth century, when the frontier had slowly but steadily pushed the Indian tribes to the west, with only a minor pause at the time of the Civil War. The missions, like the ones at San Antonio (6) and Goliad, dated from the days of the Spaniards, when they were generally associated with the forts known as *presidios*. It was on these missions that the Texan cattle industry was first developed, and the specialized beasts known as" longhorns" were bred. Slightly in mockery of the longhorn, image of the University of Texas at Austin, our campus newspaper was known as *The Shorthorn*.

(6) Pat with John Roach at the Governor's Palace in San Antonio.

Very far to the west lay the Chisos Mountains and the Rio Grande, where we once went camping, towing our little pop-up with the Mitsubishi Diamante (7). Due south of

(7) Our Mitsubishi Diamante in the park below part of the Chisos Mountains in West Texas; we are towing the camper.

Arlington, one came to the Gulf of Mexico, stretching from the Rio Grande in the west to Galveston in the east. To our surprise, most of this coast had escaped the developmental blight of states like Florida, where it can be quite difficult to reach the sea past the serried ranks of condominiums. Along the Texas coast were many parks and wildlife refuges, including particularly Aransas Pass, home of the spectacular whooping cranes. Here too, in the neighborhood of Victoria, were the remains excavated from the expedition of Robert Cavelier de La Salle, whose eventually disastrous venture of 1684 had incited French and Spanish expansion along the coast at the end of the seventeenth century. It was very evocative, to see cannon and other artefacts which had lain unknown in a Texan lagoon and prairie since the days of Louis XIV.

(8) Black Skimmers on the beach at Rockport, on the Gulf of Mexico.

The best time to see birds on the Texas coast was on really misty days, when they would forsake the ocean and congregate on the shoreline, like these Black Skimmers (8) on the beach at Rockport. The assembly of so many disparate birds in one place offered an unforgettable sight.

Some of our strangest adventures occurred when we were returning north to Chicago, at the end of the year. One year we drove through St Louis and decided to have our picnic lunch in a fairly remote site by a bayou of the Mississippi, where there were a few aged fishermen. As we ate our lunch, a hundred yards or so down a dirt road, I kept seeing late-model cars, driven by smart-looking young men, passing along the main road leading to our site. When we finished our lunch and drove off north, I saw in the mirror that one of these spiffy cars was following us, which it did for ten miles or so, and then peeled off. Thinking it over, we concluded that we had received the attentions of some drug enforcement agency (whose agents sometimes use confiscated cars), which eventually concluded from their onboard computer that our large wagon, owned by a history professor, was probably not in fact carrying drugs along the well-travelled route from Texas to Chicago.

Another time we stopped for the night in Memphis. We did not have any good idea of where to stay, but when we saw a convenient Motel Six decided to pull in there. The lodging was a little tatty, and there was no sign of the advertised restaurant, so we had supper at a nearby McDonald's. When we came to leave in the morning, pulling our camper, we were surprised that as we drew out of the hotel's park, a police cruiser barred our way. The policeman jumped out in a state of agitation: "Do you know where you are?" he said. "This here is Beirut-on-the-Mississippi, and I would advise you not to come this way again." Sobered, we drove on.

In the United States, conventional ideas of retirement have largely been given up, and it is regarded as "ageism" to suggest that people should retire at a certain age. This seems a doubly unfortunate policy, for not only are professors tempted to teach on long after they have lost their early dash, but the ladder of promotions gets hopelessly clogged, so that at the bottom end "adjuncts" serve on long after they could reasonably have hoped to enter the tenure track. I had in effect entered semi-retirement in 2000, when I accepted Oxford University Press's offer to spend half the year editing their proposed *Companion to World Exploration*. By 2006 I had reached the age of 72, the *Companion* was far advanced, and it was time to leave Texas. With some difficulty, we sold our little house, and the Department put on a delightful farewell party, giving us a splendid bowl from the University's renowned glass-foundry. Now we returned to Skokie, and I to the carrel in the Newberry that I had never abandoned.

Conclusion

Life in Retirement

The Newberry proved the perfect base for further projects. My old French colleague Bernard Barbiche (several times at the Newberry to teach their course in French paleography), having finished editing a massive inventory of Sully's possessions, was willing to resume our joint publication of Sully's memoirs. Here I could take up again the initial transcription of the manuscript material, as well as writing notes for themes that I know well, such as the development of fortifications, and relations with countries like England and Spain. Our fourth volume was published by the *Société de l'Histoire de France* in 2019; meanwhile, I adopted the tactic described by Alec Guiness in his memoir: "When I am asked, which is often, if I have retired, I am inclined to assume a pained expression and deny it."

Another project was a substantial commented catalogue of the maps of Florida. The animator of the Tampa Bay History Center there, Thomas Touchton, had over the years assembled a fine collection of historical maps of Florida, and he took advantage of the Tampa meeting of the Society for the History of Discoveries in 2013 to put on an exhibition of these maps. *Florida, the Land of Flowers* was well received, with various very effective spin-offs for schools. It was to have been accompanied by an extensive catalogue, which I largely wrote, and which should one day be a substantial contribution to the history of mapmaking in Florida. Because of various problems in Tampa, work on this catalogue has not yet come to fruition.

A more expeditious project was an edition of the Taylor Manuscript, a long account of Jamaica in 1687, now preserved at the National Library of

Jamaica. I had been working on this edition since our days at the University of the West Indies, but had been hampered by the need to decypher fuzzy microfilm. The coming of computerized imagery changed all that, making it possible to establish an entirely reliable text from these images. *Jamaica in 1687* was published in 2008, by the Press of UWI and The Mill Press (1). It aroused some controversy about the reliability of Taylor's accounts of the creatures found in the Jamaica of his day, but also proved extremely useful in providing visual and textual evidence for the site of a pirate ship, *The Golden Fleece,* on which archeologists were working in the waters of the Dominican Republic. As a further spin-off, information from the Taylor Manuscript contributed to Robert Kurson's 2015 work called *Pirate Hunters,* for a time on the New York Times bestseller list.

(1) Dust-jacket of *Jamaica in 1687* (Kingston, 2008).

The Oxford Companion to World Exploration came to fruition during the early years of my retirement. We had called on most of the necessary experts for our entries, though some refused, on the grounds that it was not a money-making venture for them. The critics received our work well, though one complained that we had not taken into account explorations by non-literate peoples, which was no doubt true if a rather impractical idea. At least the images were powerful, for to those generated from the Newberry's holdings were added a series of maps commissioned by OUP's excellent in-house cartographer (2).

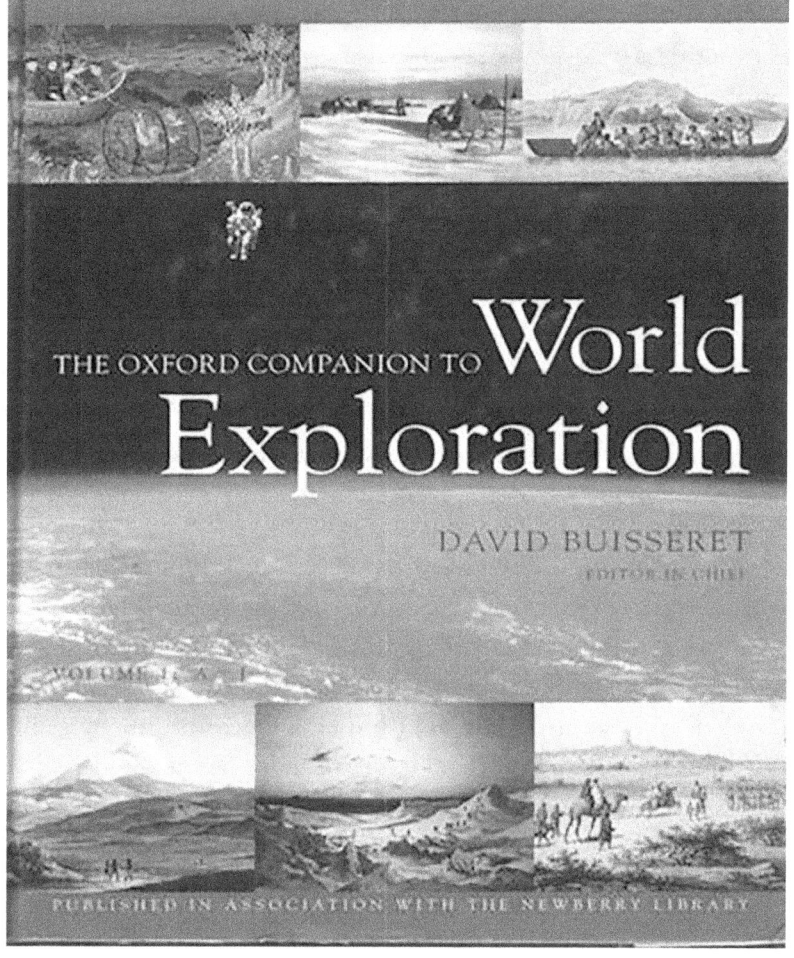

(2) Dust-jacket of *The Oxford Companion to World Exploration* (New York, 2007).

Having given up the general editorship of *Terrae Incognitae* when I left UTA in 2006, I took over as its book-review editor, continuing to use the Newberry as its institutional address. We generally succeed in providing forty or so reviews for the three yearly volumes of *TI*. The new editors have widened the review's coverage to include such areas as women explorers and the geography of the Moslem lands; they also mean to use the meetings of the Society for the History of Discoveries to generate volumes on specific themes, as opposed to my rather scattershot approach.

Retirement was a time to approach new intellectual interests. I became painfully aware of my ignorance of the natural sciences and did my best to correct this. My basis was a book called *Science* by the great popularizer Jacob Bronowski, published in 1960. Beginning from this beautifully-illustrated work, I could think about all the developments since that time: the quarks and leptons of Fermilab, the helical structure of DNA, the notion of continental drift (for both continents and for creatures) the imagery of the Hubble space-telescope, space travel; in short, the second Scientific Revolution of our time. Whereas lawyers and historians have still been using the types of evidence and arguments inherited from times past, in the natural sciences all has been turned upside-down in my day. I found it very exciting to follow these developments, if only at a considerable distance, and to reflect that in my books using aerial imagery (in the works on Jamaica, Illinois and Texas) I had at least touched on the edges of them.

There were other puzzles. Left-handed myself, I had been struck by the way in which so many of the cartographers who used the Smith Center were left-handed. What if anything did this mean? Are right-brain dominant people like this particularly drawn to occupations and themes involving spatial perception? This seemed to account for left-handedness among military pilots, for instance, but what about our left-handed recent presidents in the United States? Does this characteristic lead to an enhanced perception of the world as a whole, as opposed to the logical but limited fields offered to the left-dominant world? This phenomenon still seems to have no generally-accepted explanation, in spite of the fascinating speculations of authors like the late and much missed Oliver Sacks (*The Man who Mistook his Wife for a Hat...*).

In retirement, I began as well to reflect on the psychological problems of migration. As one author puts it, this necessarily involves the "burying of the old self," and the nurturing of a new persona. Curiously, I did not feel this as a problem in Jamaica. Pat and I were of course busy with the children, but we also seemed able to integrate ourselves more fully into the local society than was the case in the United States; here the old self had been buried, but a new one refused to come to life. In fact, the whole process of our immigration to the United States presented disadvantages that I had not at first appreciated. Some people seamlessly fitted into the new society. The historian Simon Schama, for instance, Cambridge man of a decade later than I, describes how he and his children rapidly came to enjoy baseball, and had no difficulty in entering into the other amusements of a new Yankee. I made efforts to encourage our children to follow the same path, but, like me, they remained unattracted by games like baseball and American football, and found satisfaction instead in European pastimes like soccer, gymnastics and tennis. This alienation from the sports followed by most of one's fellow-citizens is more trying than it at first seems. Watching sports stores the mind with images of great plays; Don Bradman slashing the ball through the fielders, for instance, or Colin Washbrook's ballet-like fielding at cover-point. If you no longer watch the sports of your youth, these inspiring archetypes fade away.

We did have a ready-made community of like-minded friends at the Newberry. But the demands of life in a great city meant that nothing like the after-hours community found in great universities could exist, as we all dispersed after the working day to our distant suburbs. There, the very heterogenous nature of our neighbors meant that our contacts, though friendly, could never be more than superficial since we had so few experiences in common. Moreover, men's societies tended to revolve around pursuits which were foreign to me: going to games of football and basketball, for instance, or playing golf.

As time went by, those things which I had most admired in the United States tended to be held in less esteem. The wonderful system of national parks, for instance, was more and more starved of funds, as were the public universities. In the latter case, the result was that universities, so far from being, as I had hoped and expected, engines of social mobility, tended to consolidate the grip of the wealthy, so that in the United States it was rarer than in Europe – even England – for poor children to attend the best of them. In general, it often seemed that after about 1980 private interests were favored at the expense of the public weal. For instance, the monopoly of the US Mail, which had admittedly allowed a good deal of inefficiency, tended to be eroded as the more profitable routes were taken over by private companies. In visual terms this was reflected in the fact that Post Offices were now sometimes housed in temporary-looking store fronts, instead of the substantial and often elegant buildings of former times. In the terms of theology, this was an outward sign of an inward fall from public grace.

There seemed as well to be a reversion towards what Tony Judt called "ostentatious patriotism," exemplified by the playing of the national anthem before symphony concerts. Neglecting the lesson of Vietnam, a substantial majority of our fellow-citizens supported Mr. Bush's ill-omened war in Iraq. Encouraged by the leaders of virtually all the Christian churches, Pat and I joined marches against the war in both Chicago and Dallas (3). But the United States could not muster anything like the massive protest crowds of London, which of course were equally ignored by the political leadership.

In fact, from having once imagined that I might perhaps join the British armed forces, I became in the end a more or less systematic pacifist. I was powerfully influenced on this track by a book by a particularly coherent captain of US Marines, a graduate of Princeton University called Nathaniel Fink. He explained notably that having been carefully trained to lead his men with prudence and care both for them and for the civilian populace, he found that under the pressure of combat he was forced to ask his men to behave with foolish rashness, and without due regard for what has come to be called "collateral damage." I conclude that however good the intentions at the start of hostilities, wars always develop in this way, and this brutality generally leads to stalemate at best. As Robert Southey once put it:

UNITED FOR PEACE
FAITHFUL CITIZENSHIP

hics by Lawrence Hall Youth Services
apeutic Day School Students, Episcopal
vitra-Chicago Diocese

PEACE VIGIL
ST JAMES CATHEDRAL
65 E. HURON CHICAGO, IL
December 15, 2002

3:30pm

(3) Pamphlet from the Peace Vigil at Saint James' cathedral, 2002.

"It was the British, Kasper said,

Who put the French to rout,

But what they fought each other for

I could not well make out.

'But everybody said,' quoth he,

'That 'twas a famous victory."

Curiously, I came more and more to admire the example of the Germans, whom so many of my family had spent so long fighting. The English, in contrast, seemed to have developed a particular skill for imitating the worst features of the modern United States; they gave up manufacturing things for the delights of shifting paper in the city, imitated our most tasteless television, and finally have come to rival us in social immobility. By contrast, the Germans more resembled the English of my youth; they maintained an enviable reputation for sound and innovative engineering (in spite of the recent VW scandal), exerted a fair degree of control over their banking system, and developed an education process in which social promotion was possible. They even resisted the Anglo tendency for half the population to become obese, and they refused to follow us in bellicose ventures like the ones in Iraq and Afghanistan.

Of course, the modern United States has its admirable features, not the least the way in which we continue to be able to absorb people from a wide variety of cultures. Chicago, moreover, quite transformed itself from the grubby city that I had first known in 1960. The visionary Burnham Plan of 1909 was never fully carried out, but at least the lakefront continued to be protected, so that it now forms a long parkland with a few offshore islands and fifteen long miles of uninterrupted space for walkers, cyclists, and birds. Inland, the forest preserves offer long stretches of parkland and forest, often beautifully maintained, and planted out with trees as they are needed. Indeed, Pat and I would sometimes joke, as we walked by ourselves in one of these huge parks, that we felt like some ducal couple inspecting their estate, with its well-mown lawns and well-chosen clumps of trees, the work of some latter-day Capability Brown. Plate 4 shows one of these parks (the diagonal) by our house, laid out on the site of land formerly belonging to the Potawatomi chief Billy Caldwell, alongside the North Branch of the Chicago River; it notably contains a large area of prairie restoration.

Some of the richest local habitats came about by accident, like the state park that emerged from a huge abandoned munitions-depot, to the south of Chicago. Another, the so-called "magic hedge," is a center for migratory birds that established itself on a long-abandoned Nike missile site on the lake near central Chicago. Birds find this an ideal resting-place during their long flights, north in spring and south in fall.

(4) Google Earth of part of the Forest Preserve, 2015.

Cycling has hugely developed, as have the paths and the flower-garden plantings along the medians of many streets. In the northern part of the city area, Skokie Marsh had been re-worked into a series of lagoons by the Civilian Conservation Corps. This body, set up by Roosevelt in the 1930s and often underappreciated, has been responsible for a huge number of projects throughout the United States, ranging in scale from the Blue Ridge Parkway in Virginia to the rose-garden at Fort Worth Botanic Garden in Texas. After the war, the Chicago Botanic Garden was developed at the northern end of the CCC's lagoons. This superb set of gardens, among whose many visitors may be heard every language under the sun, also has a developing scientific programme, ranging from the work of graduate students (often in remote parts of the world) to the encouragement of gardening by inner-city pupils.

Meanwhile the city's established institutions continue to flourish. At the Adler Planetarium, for instance, the displays have taken on a wider appeal, covering the latest discoveries in space, and universities like Loyola and De Paul hugely developed, becoming good examples of the seductive urban campus. When one had visitors from overseas, they were unfailingly astonished by the greening of our old industrial center. The "city of big shoulders," hog-butcher to the world, has given way to a centre for cultural and medical institutions, set in a wealth of trees and flower-beds. It remains, alas, a place where many neighbourhoods in the city experience an almost unimaginable level of gun violence, and this shows no signs of diminishing.

In the summer of 2007 we had invited Claire and her children and Paul to join us for a family holiday by the sea in North Carolina, and this gave us the idea to organize a reunion of this kind every summer. In 2011, for instance, we all met at Rowley's Bay in Wisconsin. By then we had a little sailing-boat, which we towed to the Bay and docked there for convenient sailing and fishing (5). This bay had been an early site of continental penetration by the seventeenth-century French Jesuits, and at the end of the stay we had our photograph taken beneath the remains of the cross that marked the site of the mission (6). In other years we assembled in other places: at Smith Mountain Lake in Virginia, at the Boundary Waters in far northern Minnesota, at Solomon's Island in Chesapeake Bay, and at Lake Lure in the mountains of North Carolina. When we were at Solomon's Island we were joined by Yura, daughter of Tim and Mira in Bulgaria. After that venture she came with us to Chicago for a while; she has now almost finished her studies in architecture at the University of Nantes in western France.

(5) Tom and Paul take *Serendipity* out at Rowley's Bay, 2011.

(6) The family at Rowley's Bay, 2011.

In 2012 we visited Colorado, to attend the wedding of Paul and Kelly Oshetski. The ceremony took place in the garden of Kelly's mother, Linda, at Longmont just under the front range of the Rockies, and we had our wedding lunch at a local hotel. Plate 7 shows Kelly talking to my brother Kit on that occasion, and plate 8 shows Paul in conversation with his eldest brother, Tim, who had come from Bulgaria. Paul and Kelly settled in the Denver area, where he worked as a primary care physician for Kaiser Permanente, and she as a "hospitalist", which is a new medical specialty involving the continuing care of a great variety of patients newly arrived in a hospital. They have two children, Ellis and Julia.

(7) Kelly Oshetski and Kit at her wedding in Colorado, 2012.

(8) Tim and Paul at the Colorado wedding, 2012.

With children and grandchildren in Bulgaria, Virginia, Memphis and Denver, Pat and I generally travelled in order to visit them. Occasionally we ventured further afield. Thus in 2010 I acted as expert for a two-week cruise in the West Indies from Barbados. Pat and I occupied a crew cabin with the delightful feature of a couple of portholes, and visited many different islands, some of which I knew from forty years earlier (9). Unfortunately, the ship was not geared so much for lectures as for bingo; nevertheless, I did succeed in steadily expanding my audience, and could see that well-designed lectures could add greatly to the enjoyment of such a cruise.

(9) David on a visit to the Botanic Garden at Saint Vincent, 2010.

Sometimes, too, we went on ventures with Pat's sister Margie and her husband Damon. In 2000 we rented a house on the Yucatán Peninsula in Mexico, at Playa del Carmen. At that time this area was relatively underdeveloped, and we alternated between the beach and visits to inland Maya sites, using a mini-bus that we rented. Some years later we made a rather similar visit to the Dominican Republic, beginning in the splendid capital of Santo Domingo, with its strong echoes of Columbus, and ending up on the north coast. In both Mexico and the DR, we had the feeling that the demands of mass tourism were beginning to outstrip the reasonable use of natural resources.

We even had this feeling, to some degree, when we visited England in the summer of 2015. Again, we rented accommodation, this time in Yorkshire and in Suffolk, taking delight in buying our food in the local shops and so getting a certain feel for the country (10). England, indeed, seemed to us astonishingly prosperous after our days there around 1960; the roads were full of new cars, and people seemed to eat out very often. Cambridge seemed, though, rather like some of the little ports that we knew in the Caribbean, to have been overwhelmed by the number of visitors. It was sad to see that in order to stem this flow of visitors, colleges had to charge for entry, rather like attractions in some Disney Park.

(10) Pat with Marge and Damon at Fountains Abbey, 2015.

In 2018, we organized our summer reunion at Dandridge, where a lake had been formed in the course of the work of the Tennessee Valley Authority. Here, alas, catastrophe befell us. Some of the children were all swimming together with their children (the rest of us were in the town), and Paul somehow got into difficulty. He was an accomplished waterman, capable of flipping a kayak, but on this occasion seems to have suffered from some kind of attack. The others furiously dived down to recover him but were too late. We held a memorial for him the following June, at which I chiefly remember the tears of an aged patient of his, who still could hardly believe that his "Dr. B." was gone forever. We received a good many unexpected letters from people who remembered his various acts of kindness.

Back in Skokie, we did our best to absorb this shock. Perhaps we were a little comforted by the words of Tacitus, who once wrote that if you have a garden and a library, you have all that you could need. We tried to think of Paul in our domestic tasks. For instance, we expanded the garden; Pat looked after the flowers, with a particular interest in Midwest plants, and in those that would attract bees and butterflies. We succeeded in establishing a patch of milkweed, part of similar plantings stretching in a corridor from Mexico to Canada, in order to encourage the superb monarch butterfly in its seasonal migrations. I developed a vegetable garden, growing not only the standard beans, squash and tomatoes, but also relatively unusual crops like leeks, kale and arugula. The land is fertile, having once been part of a farmer's field; indeed, you could still see some of the large trees that had marked the field-boundaries. At first, too, a few of the farms survived, but by the end of the twentieth century all had disappeared.

(11) The garden at 5126 Lunt Avenue, 2018.

Our house was too far inland fully to benefit from the annual migrations of the birds, but we did have periodic visitors, in particular the northern flicker, a sort of woodpecker who often called to rummage on our lawn both on his/her way north in the spring and then on the way back south in the fall. Of course, we also had many residents, ranging from the sparrows who spent the cold days deep in the forsythia bush, to the handsome red cardinal and his dowdy wife, the raucous blue jay and the woodpeckers (both Downy and Golden-breasted) who would sometimes come and tap on the rotting wood of our pergola, looking for tasty insects. Sometimes, too, we would be visited by large red-tailed hawks, in search of easy pickings at our feeders (11).

When Tacitus spoke of a library, he surely had in mind physical books. But for the past quarter-century it has been possible both to read books and to compose books and articles on a home computer. Even more astonishing is the way that one can now call up the contents of individual libraries throughout the world, check what they hold by using the consolidated list known as "WorldCat," and even order printed books. From the historian's point of view, the only remaining problem comes in the need to consult distant manuscript archives. A few have been put on line, but for most archival research the use of microfilm still seems best – an example of a remarkably durable technology, for fifty-year-old reels generally survive entirely intact, and can be read with simple viewers.

To the garden and library, we ought to add music. It is extraordinary to think that a little over one hundred years ago, any form of music had to be created on the spot. Then came a sequence of devices: first the radio, then vinyl records, then tapes, then CDs and now downloads from the internet. This profusion of music is surely one of the most astonishing developments in the lives of people all over the world. We now take for granted a feature of everyday life that would have been beyond the wildest imaginings of the most powerful monarchs of former times.

Of course, Chicago is also still abundantly supplied with live music as well, from groups like the Chicago Symphony, the orchestras of Northwestern University or the players of Music of the Baroque. Pat and I have particularly appreciated the recitals of the Newberry Consort, which specializes in playing music taken from often unknown scores preserved at the Library, such as the hymns composed by the nuns of a convent in sixteenth-century Mexico City. We have also enjoyed the astonishing combination of early modern music and contemporary imagery offered by the Tafelmusik Baroque Orchestra of Toronto. We sang ourselves for many years in the choir of Saint Peter's church, where we were just in time to hear the final echoes of the great German choirs which existed there until the Second World War.

Saint Pete's, as it is called, has played a considerable part in our lives at Skokie. In a history written with some fellow-parishioners I have described its transformation from a small parish established by German and Luxembourg truck-farmers into a multi-ethnic church, with parishioners from every corner of the world. Some of these faith-traditions have strongly influenced our liturgy, like the work coming out of the ecumenical community at Taizé in France. Occasionally hymns will hark back to the great poets of the sixteenth and seventeenth century, like Marvell and Donne, as well as later works like those of Ralph Vaughan Williams. I also remain wedded to the *Oxford Book of English Verse,* where so much of this poetry may be found.

These works are all the more powerful when the words can be related to some place, notably like a country churchyard. I particularly savor the words of Tennyson, whom I imagine composing "Crossing the Bar" as he rambled on the green downs of the Isle of Wight above the English Channel, near the place that I was born:

Sunset and evening star

And one clear call for me...

Twilight and evening bell

And after that the dark

And may there be no sadness of farewell

When I embark.

I.W. Wotton, *Alum Bay, Isle of Wight* (London, 1840).
Tennyson's Down is above the Bay.

List of Books Used or Cited

1. Baden-Powell, Sir Robert. *Scouting for Boys: A Handbook for Instruction in Good Citizenship* (first published 1908: Oxford, 2004).

2. Belloc, Hilaire. *The Path to Rome* (first published 1904: Chicago, 1954). A charming account of a journey (in both senses) to Rome.

3. Blythe, Ronald. *Akenfield: Portrait of an English Village* (New York, 1969). Convincing portrait of the hard life of Suffolk villagers in the 1930s.

4. Botton, Alain de. *The Art of Travel* (New York, 2003). Reflections on the importance of the countryside to spiritual well-being.

5. Buchan, John. *Pilgrim's Way; An Essay in Recollection* (Cambridge, MA, 1940). The novelist and statesman reflects on his life in the British Empire.

6. Cathcart, Brian. *The Fly in the Cathedral* (New York, 2004). Excellent summary of early research into the atom.

7. Bronowski, Jacob. *Science* (New York, 1960). Beautifully-illustrated summary of scientific knowledge just after the Second World War.

8. Collingwood, R. *The Idea of History* (Oxford, 1946). Influential reflections on the role of the observer in historical writing.

9. Collinson, Patrick. *The History of a History Man* (Woodbridge, 2011). An eminent historian reflects on his life and times.

10. Dalrymple, Theodore. *Our Culture, What's Left of It* (Chicago, 2005). A doctor's regretful assessment of England in the late twentieth century.

11. Deighton, Len. *Fighter: The True Story of the Battle of Britain* (London, 1977). Excellent summary of the Battle of Britain and what led up to it.

12. Dickens, Charles. *The Posthumous Papers of the Pickwick Club* (First published 1837, New York, 1938). Ipswich adventures, near Woodbridge.

13. Fink, Nathaniel. *One Bullet Away* (Boston/New York, 2005). A captain of Marines reflects on the nature of modern infantry warfare.

14. Fleming, Peter. *Operation Sealion* (New York, 1957). Captures the irrational confidence felt in England after the fall of France in 1940.

15. Galbraith, J.K. *A Life in Our Times* (Boston, 1981). A clear-eyed if disabused look at recent Western history.

16. Hager, Thomas. *The Demon under the Microscope* (New York, 2006). A revealing account of the emergence of "M and B," precursor of penicillin.

17. Halferin, Gerald. *Humboldt's Cosmos* (New York, 2004). Particularly strong on Humboldt's time in the New World.

18. Hemingway, Ernest. *A Moveable Feast* (New York, 1964). Reflections on his days in Paris, his "moveable feast."

19. Henty, G.A. *Under Drake's Flag: A Tale of the Spanish Main* (London, 1882). Victorian imperial confidence.

20. Hitchens, Peter. *The Abolition of Britain: from Winston Churchill to Princess Diana* (San Francisco, 2000). A disabused account of these years in Great Britain.

21. Huxley, Elspeth. *The Flame Trees of Thika* (London, 1959). Evocative account of an African childhood.

22. Jackson, J.B. *American Space* (New York, 1972). Reflections on the historical landscape in the United States.

23. Jones, R.V. *The Wizard War* (New York, 1978). Interesting account of early Bawdsey and the development of radar.

24. Judt, Tony. *The Memory Chalet* (New York, 2010). Dying reflections by this eminent historian.

25. Judt, Tony. *Ill Fares the Land* (New York, 2010). This verse continues "to hastening ills a prey, where wealth accumulates and men decay;" Judt offers a sharp criticism of the modern United States.

26. Kubler, George. *The Shape of Time* (New Haven, 1962). Insightful reflections on the nature of historical development, and the importance of studies "on the fringe."

27. Lamartine, Alphonse de. *Recueillements poétiques* (Paris, 1954). The poems of this irresible Romantic poet.

28. Lax, Eric. *The Mold in Dr. Florey's Coat* (New York, 2004). Explains Dr. Heatley's crucial role in the development of penicillin.

29. Maryatt, Captain. *Peter Simple, or the Adventures of a Midshipman* (1837).

30. McGilchrist, Iain. *The Master and the Emissary: the Divided Brain and the Making of the Western World* (Yale, 2009). Far-reaching claims about the significance of "handedness."

31. *The Oxford Book of English Verse* (first published 1900; many subsequent editions).

32. Palgrave, Francis. *The Golden Treasury* (first published 1981; New York, 1964). A collection of poems that well accompanies *The Oxford Book of English Verse.*

33. Ransome, Arthur. *Swallows and Amazons* (first published 1930; Boston, 1938).

34. Rhodes, Richard. *The Making of the Atomic Bomb* (New York, 1986). Full and readable account of the coming of the atomic age.

35. Sachs, Oliver. *The Man Who Mistook his Wife for a Hat* (New York, 1985). Part of a series of reflections on the nature of the brain.

36. Sheffield, Charles. *Earthwatch: A Survey of the World from Space* (New York, 1981). An early example of the historical and ecological use of aerial imagery.

37. Stuart, Andrea. *Sugar in the Blood: A Family's Story of Slavery and Empire* (New York, 2012). Reflections on the early history of the University of the West Indies.

38. Thornhill, Michael. *Road to Suez: the Battle of the Canal Zone* (Stroud, 2006). Background to the occupation of the Canal Zone.

39. Townsend, Peter. *Duel of Eagles* (New York, 1970). Enlightening account of the Battle of Britain by a leading participant.

40. Waugh, Evelyn. *Sword of Honour* (Boston, 1966). The Second World War, seen through Waugh's sardonic eyes.

41. Wordsworth, William. *The Poetical Works of William Wordsworth* (Oxford, 1940). A poet who early saw our present ecological discontents.

Index

www.ingramcontent.com/pod-product-compliance
Lightning Source LLC
Chambersburg PA
CBHW071723120626
46550CB00001B/355